PASTORAL CARE WITH CHILDREN IN CRISIS

Published by The Westminster Press

By Andrew D. Lester
Pastoral Care with Children in Crisis
Coping with Your Anger: A Christian Guide

By Andrew D. and Judith L. Lester
Understanding Aging Parents (Christian Care Books)

Edited by Gerald L. Borchert and Andrew D. Lester
Spiritual Dimensions of Pastoral Care:
Witness to the Ministry of Wayne E. Oates

PASTORAL CARE WITH CHILDREN IN CRISIS

Andrew D. Lester

Westminster John Knox Press
Louisville, Kentucky

Scripture quotations from the Revised Standard Version
of the Bible are copyrighted 1946, 1952, © 1971, 1973
by the Division of Christian Education of the National
Council of the Churches of Christ in the U.S.A. and are
used by permission.

Book design by Christine Schueler

First edition

Published by The Westminster Press®
Philadelphia, Pennsylvania

PRINTED IN THE UNITED STATES OF AMERICA
9   8   7

Library of Congress Cataloging in Publication Data

Lester, Andrew D.
    Pastoral care with children in crisis.

    Bibliography: p.
    Includes index.
    1. Church work with children. I.Title.
BV639.C4L37 1985   253.5   84-21901
ISBN 0-664-24598-6 (pbk.)

To my children
SCOTT AND DENISE

Who provided insight into Jesus' saying,

*"Unless you turn and become like children,
you will never enter the kingdom of heaven"*
(Matthew 18:3)

CONTENTS

ACKNOWLEDGMENTS

Many persons have provided the support, encouragement, academic stimulation, and professional dialogue that is so necessary for writing a book. I am grateful to the trustees of the Southern Baptist Theological Seminary, President Roy L. Honeycutt, and Walter B. Shurden, former Dean of the School of Theology, for providing and funding the sabbatical program that made possible a year of concentrated research and writing.

My friend Bernard Weisskopf, M.D., Director of the Child Evaluation Center of the Department of Pediatrics at the University of Louisville School of Medicine, graciously provided office space and support services during this sabbatical year. He and the staff created a cordial, yet private, environment which was ideal for research and writing.

To write this book it was necessary to involve myself again in pastoral work with children in crisis. Several persons provided such an opportunity. Rev. R. Wayne Willis, Pediatrics Chaplain in the Department of Pastoral Care at Kosair-Children's Hospital, arranged for me to work on the chaplain's staff, offering both colleagueship and considerable expertise with children. Carrie White, an expressive therapist, introduced me to several of the methodologies developed in this book. Dr. Salvatore Bertolone, M.D., Chief of Hematology-Oncology in the Department of Pediatrics, included me in his rounds on the pediatric oncology unit. Kathy Michael, R.N., a nurse specialist in the same department, was very astute in her understanding of children.

Further exposure to children in crisis was provided by the Children's Program of Hospice of Louisville, Inc. Patricia B. Howard, Associate Director for Patient Care, Jackie Miller, R.N., and Nancy Lange, R.N., accepted me as a colleague and shared with me their perceptions and experiences.

Four students, David Coleman, Susie Cossey, Dwayne Howell, and Daniel Johnston, were interested in pastoral care to children and worked with me for a semester. We met one hour a week to discuss both their academic research and their practical experiences with the children to whom they were ministering. I appreciate their enthusiastic contribution to this endeavor.

It was important to have consultation from professionals who study childhood, know children, and work with them in a variety of roles. A number of friends and colleagues qualified as such experts. They are pastors, child psychologists, professors, child care specialists, chaplains, pastoral counselors, and family therapists. They generously read large portions of the early editions, and many of their valuable suggestions are incorporated in this final copy. Thank you Dan Aleshire, Clarence Barton, Mary Barton, Kay Byrd, Claudia Crawford, Bob Dever, Polly Dillard, Craig Dykstra, John Edgar, Ed Hampe, Ron Higdon, James Hyde, Steve Ivy, Len Jepson, Bill McKain, Jim Pollard, Wade Rowatt, Steve Shoemaker, Randy Simmonds, Anne Smith, Edward Thornton, and Wayne Willis. Going the second mile with their time and energy were Kathryn Chapman and Wayne Oates.

It has been a pleasure to work again with Cynthia Thompson, editor at Westminster Press. She combines affirmation, patience, editorial suggestions, and gentle prodding into a perfect motivational mix.

My wife, Judy, once again gave loving support and encouragement through this entire process.

INTRODUCTION

Let me share with you why I have committed time and energy to the subject of pastoral care with children. The experiences that led me to write this book may be quite similar to the experiences that motivate you to read it.

When I served as a rural pastor, I enjoyed my relationship with the children. I was particuarly close with one five-year-old girl, whom we will call Janice. She and I looked forward to seeing each other on Sundays and on occasion during the week. One Sunday I noticed that she treated me with caution, refusing even to smile in my direction or respond to my greeting. I shrugged it off as one of those "she got up on the wrong side of the bed" days. But when this same thing occurred the second Sunday, I became concerned (I don't like to be rejected, especially by children!). That afternoon I made a visit to the family's home with the purpose of finding out what had caused this breach in our relationship. Janice wanted no part of me during this visit either. During the conversation I described my concern to the mother, a very sweet and thoughtful person in her mid-twenties. Part of her response included this stunning statement:

> I can't imagine what's come over Janice. She likes and admires you so much and would do just anything you asked. In fact, several weeks ago I had to discipline her

so often that I told her I was going to tell *you* she was
being a bad girl and that you would tell God. I said if she
wanted you and God to like her again, she had better quit
misbehaving and be a good girl.

Needless to say, the mother and I had some intense conversation about my role as a pastor and the nature of God's response to five-year-olds. Then we called Janice in and communicated to her that both God and I were glad when she was
a good girl, but that our love for her was too strong for her
to break by misbehaving. She finally got the message that our
relationship was special, whatever happened at home. Her
good-by smile and hug I will never forget. But the incident left
me wondering about the variety of ways in which children
view the pastor and how these perceptions affect their view of
God. We will return to this issue in chapter 2.

Not long after this event, I entered my first clinical pastoral
education program in Louisville, Kentucky, to discover that I
had been assigned to Children's Hospital (now Kosair-Children's Hospital). Though young and relatively inexperienced,
I was expected to take pastoral responsibility for a hospital full
of children, many of whom were seriously ill. Neither my
seminary education nor two years as a pastor had prepared me
for this. The first weeks of that experience are burned into my
memory. I was overwhelmed by children who were in pain,
frightened, alone, and angry. When they looked *to* me I felt
inadequate; when they looked *away* from me I felt like a
failure. I did not know what they were thinking or how to talk
with them. How I wished for a book about pastoral care with
children in crisis!

Several years later I was busily preparing to teach my first
courses as an instructor in the Psychology of Religion and
Pastoral Care department at the Southern Baptist Theological
Seminary. One was the introductory course called "The Ministry of Pastoral Care." I intended to use personality theories
and developmental psychology as a backdrop for helping the
students discover appropriate ways and means to give pastoral
care at various ages and stages of the human life cycle, including pastoral intervention in life's crises. Since I had set aside

several weeks of the semester to explore the stages of child-hood, and pastoral care to children, I began to scan the litera-ture for resources. I was already aware of the extensive mate-rial (clinical research, theoretical formulations, and clinical application) written by the social and behavioral scientists.

My surprise came when I looked for material produced for the pastor. Literature concerning religion and children was focused primarily on religious education and worship. I was amazed that so little attention had been given to children by the pastoral care literature. No general textbook existed to guide pastors in relating effectively and meaningfully to chil-dren from Monday through Saturday, much less to intervene in their crises. With that realization came my first images of a book like this one. During that year, in fact, a colleague and I outlined a book we intended to write, but in a classic example of neglect, we did not get it written.

In the eighteen intervening years, my experiences have con-tinued to be a reminder of this gap in the field of pastoral care. Ministering as a chaplain and supervising clinical pastoral edu-cation students on the pediatric wards at the Baptist Medical Center in Winston-Salem, North Carolina, I was constantly aware of how difficult it was to provide quality pastoral care to the children.

Like other pastoral counselors, I am frequently reminded of the significant impact of childhood crises on an individual's later adult identity, specifically on spiritual formation. I am convinced that the negative impact of these crises could be reduced if a sensitive, knowledgeable pastor had intervened. Recently, for example, I talked with a woman in her early thirties who in the last year has recalled to consciousness a critical event that occurred when she was eight years old. She was molested sexually by a truck driver who offered her a ride to school. In therapy she has discovered how much of her selfhood (uncertainty about the nature of her sexuality, irra-tional guilt, a recurring sense of worthlessness, and being overly responsible for everyone in her care, to name a few) has been affected by that crisis, both the time she spent in the truck and the reactions of her parents and the police. Of particular interest is her clear memory that this incident caused her to question the religious teaching of her church and family that God could be trusted as Protector. Needless to say, her pastor was not involved in this crisis, and no one knew of her spiritual struggle.

Last, but certainly not least, I have helped parent two children through the preadolescent years. As they let me share in their pilgrimage, I have been aware of the many points where pastoral care either was or would have been meaningful.

I have written this book, then, because experiences like those I have shared above convince me that (1) children have crises; (2) children deserve pastoral care as much as any other members of the church; (3) the pastor's relationship with children, particularly when they are in a crisis, can have a significant impact on their spiritual growth and development; and (4) few resources have been made available to pastors that inform and guide their pastoral care with children.

It would be obvious from the foregoing that I am writing this book specifically for pastors and other ministers who claim and actualize a pastoral identity: chaplains, church staff members, professors, and so forth. I hope, however, that any person who is interested in relating more creatively to children, especially Christian parents and teachers, will profit from these ideas.

Whatever shape your ministry takes, you as a pastor are loaded with responsibilities: preaching, teaching, administering, leading, visiting, counseling, and, of course, preparing for all of these functions. The fact that you are sitting down to read this book means you are among those pastors who are determined to keep on learning and growing despite the heavy demands on your time and energy. Continuing education for the pastor, however, has its own hazards. You are bombarded with information and ideas suggesting that if you were really a faithful and effective pastor, you would spend twenty hours a week doing whatever it is that the author or speaker thinks is a priority. You have even been the target of those who seek to induce a guilt trip if you do not jump on their bandwagon.

I am trying to walk a middle ground. It is clear to me, on the one hand, that all your ministry functions are important, so I do not intend to call for a radical change in your priorities or use of time. On the other hand, I am trying to heighten your consciousness of an important but often overlooked focus of ministry. I will be trying to persuade you to add a perspective to your ministry, to raise the pastoral care of children in crisis higher on your list of priorities. Since you probably cannot add anything to your schedule, I must present my case in such a manner that you would be willing to make a slight realignment of how you expend your time and energy.

You may assume that it takes a lot of special knowledge and a high level of therapeutic competency to be effective in caring for children in crisis. If we were talking about children with identifiable mental problems and emotional disorders, you would be making an accurate assumption. However, in this book we are concerned about ministry to normal children, with no diagnosed mental problems, who are caught in crises and experiencing the normal stress and anxiety associated with being in a crisis. Please know that I am not interested in convincing you to take time off to get advanced training which would prepare you for doing pastoral psychotherapy with children. My goal is to convince you that your gifts in pastoral care can be applied to children with creative, life-changing results.

A word about age groupings and stages in life. The word "children" in everyday speech is most likely to refer to small children, those old enough to walk but not yet in school. These children are known formally as "preschoolers" and the stage as "early childhood." In this book, however, "children" refers to those between the ages of five and twelve, the period known as "middle childhood," "school age," or "preadolescence." We will be talking about ministry to those from kindergarten through sixth or seventh grade, depending on when puberty is established. What is written in the first two chapters is certainly true of all children, but as we move into the later chapters we are describing ways and means of pastoral care appropriate for the school-age child.

This is an introductory book and leaves much unsaid. The more I study and work with children, the more I realize how much is yet to be done on the subject of pastoral care and children. For example, the research on intellectual and cognitive development, moral development, and faith development is yet to be applied to the pastoral care of children, even though the field of religious education has used these studies to inform and prepare church school teachers. My purpose did not leave room for such work, but it would be quite profitable to the pastor. Another example: children enjoy music, but music is not included among the methodologies described in Part II.

The four chapters in Part I discuss why children are left out of our pastoral care, why we should include them, what they need from their pastors in a time of crisis, and what the basic guidelines are for pastoral care of children. The four chapters in Part II describe the use of play, storytelling, art, and writing in facilitating pastoral conversation with children in crisis. These methods of pastoral care are new and different. At first glance, they may seem to require advanced skills and training. On closer examination, however, you will realize that using these techniques may make you self-conscious, but they do not demand any special preparation. The only requirement is a willingness to try something new.

Some pastors who read early drafts of this material felt a little overwhelmed by all the possibilities. Chapters 5 through 8 seemed to call for extensive new forms of ministry. My purpose, of course, is to energize, not immobilize, so please think of Part II as a cafeteria of ideas from which to choose only a handful. Find several that seem most comfortable, fit your style of relating, and match your personal interests.

One pastor, for example, said he could not use puppets because he knew he would feel embarrassed to talk as if he were the puppet. This same pastor, however, enjoys table games and was immediately interested in putting together the Bag of Words game and purchasing the Ungame (chapter 5). Another pastor had always been interested in art and did some painting in her spare time. She could quickly envision using art activity with children (chapter 6). A third pastor declined to use any writing instruments in his pastoral care (see chapter 6) because they reminded him of his own feelings of inferiority concerning spelling and writing skills when he was a school-age child. However, he likes both to hear and to tell stories, so he feels right at home using storytelling techniques (chapter 7). You will also find some methods more inviting than others. Pick ones you can imagine using with the least amount of self-consciousness. Later, after you become more comfortable with children, other methods can be tried. The more naturally spontaneous and playful your personality, the more excited you will be about using these new tools.

One word of caution: All these methods are projective techniques. That is, they are activities that allow a person to "see" in something *outside* the self that which is actually *inside* the self. Put another way, projection means unconsciously investing portions of one's own thinking and feeling in something external to the self. Professional psychotherapists use these tools diagnostically, but the methods also enable you, as pastor, to make assessments that inform your care of children. Please remember, however, that we are not asking you to interpret any of the child's unconscious self beyond your training. These methods allow children to conceptualize and express in pastoral conversation what they are consciously thinking and feeling. From these conscious revelations you will find plenty of information to guide your pastoral care. If you think that a deeper understanding is necessary to care for a particular child, seek consultation with a professionally trained specialist.

When reading of the use of play, art, storytelling, and writing as instruments of pastoral care with children, visions of fully equipped playrooms with one-way mirrors may dance in your head. However helpful to the psychotherapist who works with children, such elaborate equipment is not necessary to the pastor as he or she ministers to children.

On the other hand, to make use of these methods you will need some props and equipment. Let me suggest in advance, therefore, that you plan to create a Children's Kit for your personal use. (Chaplain Wayne Willis introduced me to this idea.) We are talking about a simple zippered briefcase (under $10 at any discount department store) which will hold what you need. Such a kit can be kept in the trunk of your car, instead of in your office, so it will be available when you need it. (You may want to keep an identical kit in your office, but, if not, one will be in the parking lot for those times when you want to use it at church.) Specific items to include are suggested in Part II.

And now I turn the book over to you, anticipating that it can help you either begin a ministry to children or deepen the pastoral care you already offer. I am trusting, furthermore, that you (both pastors and pastoral care specialists) will write about your ministry with children (practice) and your subsequent reflections on these experiences (theory). I look forward to the time when we establish a body of literature on pastoral care and children such as we presently have on pastoral care in grief and bereavement. Meanwhile, I hope these chapters will calm your qualms and whet your appetite for ministry to children. They contain enough practical ideas that, if you read them tonight, you can use these skills tomorrow.

PART I

THE PASTOR AND CHILDREN

1

THE PASTORAL NEGLECT
OF CHILDREN

This morning the pediatrics team of our local Hospice organization met to discuss the care being provided for two terminally ill children and their families. (Hospice is an international association that helps meet the physical, social, psychological, and spiritual needs of the terminally ill and their families.) Both families were religious—one Catholic, the other Protestant. In each case both the Hospice nurse and the volunteer personally informed the priest and the pastor of the child's situation and invited them to become involved. Pastoral care would have been appropriate and meaningful to each child, yet neither the priest nor the pastor had chosen to make contact with the families. Why not?

As a volunteer chaplain/pastor, I listened to the frustrations of the Hospice staff, feeling embarrassed to be a member of the clergy, and wondered, Why haven't my colleagues in ministry responded? Because of my concern for the terminally ill children with whom I was working, plus my heightened advocacy on behalf of children, anger quickly replaced embarrassment. This anger was moderated, however, when I remembered my earliest experiences with very sick children. I have already described my first clinical training program (see Introduction), in which I was assigned to Children's Hospital. I felt particularly inadequate with children who were terminally ill. I remember the guilt I felt when I chose to cope with my anxiety

23

by avoiding situations I did not think I could handle. When we are frightened by a situation or have a strong sense of inadequacy, it is easy to avoid involvement in order to escape the anxiety. So I knew one possible reason the priest and the pastor did not come.

Let me describe another source of my concern about the pastoral care of children in crisis. For thirteen years at two different seminaries I have taught a course every semester on "Pastoral Care in Human Crisis." Students in this course may choose, as one of their research projects, to study a crisis they have experienced personally. Many students have used this opportunity to relive, better understand, and "work through" a crisis in their own past. Since seminarians are usually young adults, many of these crises occurred before adolescence. Over the years hundreds of students have written papers about their childhood crises—parents divorcing, the death of a significant person (parent, sibling, grandparent, friend), serious illness and hospitalization, abuse (physical, sexual, emotional), and all types of accidents and traumas.

In these papers each student must answer the question, "What ministry did you receive personally from your church, particularly from the pastor?" In most instances the answer is a brief "none." While reading these papers each semester, I have been staggered by the absence of Christian ministry during these childhood crises. In paper after paper the students have said, "The pastor did not know," or "The pastor never came by," or "I had no contact with the pastor during this time." They may recall that the pastor was involved with their parents and other adults during the crisis, but with few exceptions they did not experience any direct pastoral care. So I wonder—*where were the pastors?* How could these little ones in the faith have been so abandoned in their time of need?

Fear and a sense of inadequacy may explain the absence of some pastors. For others it might have been the press of time: preparing sermons, administering the church, going to meetings, visiting the hospital, teaching classes, recruiting help, raising budgets, planning weddings and funerals. Reflecting on my work as a pastor, however, I think lack of awareness was more of a reason for neglecting the children than lack of time.

When I think back on the crises with which the families in my church struggled, I can now recognize that the children were also in crisis. At that time, however, my awareness of their needs was limited. Neglect of the children, therefore, is caused not only by our inadequacy and the push of time but also by ignorance and lack of awareness about childhood crises. Let me illustrate.

Consider this typical emergency in the local parish presented in a pastoral consultation group. The pastor who shared this case is thirty-eight years of age and has been a pastor for thirteen years. He received a telephone call at eight thirty one evening from Anthony, who reported that his twelve-year marriage to Claudia was coming apart at the seams. After an intense outburst she had retreated to the local hotel for the night, saying she was through with the marriage. Anthony was very disturbed and concerned for both Claudia, alone in a hotel, and the children, who were anxious about the conflict they had witnessed and their mother's departure. This pastor talked half an hour on the telephone with Anthony and another fifteen minutes with Claudia, whom he was able to reach at the hotel. He arranged to see them individually the next day. During the following month, while Anthony and Claudia were separated, the pastor worked to help them resolve their conflict. He met with them twice a week—once individually and once conjointly. He also consulted with a local pastoral counselor by telephone, finally getting the couple referred for marital therapy. He continued to offer support to both of them by telephone and in brief conversations with Anthony at church. He also talked twice with Anthony's parents, who were members of the church, and with one of Claudia's friends who wanted to know how to help.

It was obvious to the consultation group that this pastor had spent much time and energy being a faithful, and indeed effective, pastor to this couple. Near the end of the consultation, however, the following conversation took place between myself and this pastor:

CONSULTANT: What about the children?
PASTOR: They're doing okay, I guess.

C: Tell me about them.

P: Well, the girl is almost eleven, the boy
                about nine.

C: Have you talked with either of them on
                the phone?

P: No, I haven't.

C: Have you visited the home to be specifi-
                cally with them?

P: No.

C: Have you invited them to the church to
                talk with you about how they are handling
                this?

P: No, I've never done that with children.

C: Why not?

P: I just haven't thought about it.

Since the other ministers in the consultation group were also
surprised by my questions and confessed that they too would
have overlooked the children, we spent some profitable time
examining the reasons why pastors omit children from their
awareness.

Notice what has occurred. A faithful, hardworking pastor
has made an effective response to a marital crisis. He spent time
on the telephone with both partners during the critical evening, saw each of them immediately the next day, met with
them twice a week for several weeks, arranged a referral,
continued support through telephone calls, and was involved
with the husband's parents and a friend of the wife. Yet he
never thought about the children! Why? Not because he was
insensitive, or uncaring, or busy playing golf, or hated kids. He
simply was not aware of the children's needs. Even the most
sensitive and caring pastor may not be aware of the children
in crisis.

You may feel some kinship with the pastors in this consultation group. Perhaps you have noticed that you also focus your
pastoral care on adults and find that children, for some reason,
are screened from your attention. You may be entertaining the
harsh thought that in your ministry the children have been

neglected. Avoidance may have been intentional because of anxiety over making a mistake or a sense of inadequacy about relating to children. Or your neglect may result from a simple lack of awareness. In either case, rest assured that you are not alone. Such neglect is widespread.

During the last three years, I have talked with many pastors, of various denominations, about their ministry to children. From these conversations two conclusions are obvious. First, though some pastors do involve themselves in leading children in worship, and most are concerned about providing adequate Christian education programs within their congregations, *few pastors give any systematic attention to pastoral relationships with children, even those in crisis.* Many pastors have never structured a pastoral conversation with a child, either in their office or in the child's home, with the specific goal of offering pastoral care during a crisis. How could we explain this neglect?

Second, when they do attempt to provide pastoral care for children *pastors are usually frustrated by their perception that they lack the knowledge and skills to offer such care effectively.* Pastors are not aware of resources that can assist them in relating creatively to children. What are the reasons for this sense of inadequacy? Join me in seeking out the causes of this neglect and putting an end to it. Following are some of the reasons why children are neglected by pastors.

CHILDHOOD IDEALIZED

In the last forty years, Western culture, particularly the ever-expanding middle class, has developed a tendency to romanticize childhood. Several factors contributed to this transition: (1) This country developed into a "child worshiping" culture after the depression of the 1930s; (2) the prosperity following World War II allowed families to lavish much more time, energy, and resources on their children than ever before; (3) as families moved off the farm, children did not have to work as much or as early in life; and (4) more and more full-time mothers, with the aid of labor-saving devices, began to focus most of their attention on taking care of the children, seeing that all the needs of the child were met plus all the extras—

piano lessons, dance lessons, and extracurricular activities at school.

Society took notice of all these changes and began to idealize childhood as the golden age of innocence, a time of cookies and lemonade, all fun and play, nothing to worry about. The pastor who is caught up in this cultural view of childhood may unwittingly overlook the fact that children experience fears, anxieties, embarrassments, self-doubts, blows to self-esteem, heartaches, grief, guilt, shame, resentments, and other inner turmoil.

Also contributing to this idealization of childhood is our tendency, even our need, to "forget" the inner turmoil that we experienced as children. Paying attention to the heartaches of the children in our parish may remind us of the painful heart-aches from our own past. Since we try to protect ourselves from that pain, it is no wonder that we conveniently block from our awareness that today's children are going through the same critical experiences mentioned above.

How Children Communicate

Children do not communicate their concerns and emotional pain in the same manner as adults. They aren't practiced at conceptualizing how they feel and what they think. Therefore, they do not know how to let us know directly that they are in crisis.

Children often use play as a method of processing their thoughts and feelings as they cope with crises. This play activity is the normal context in which children live out their lives, but adults tend to assume that if the child was really grieved over her father's death, she would not be playing tag outside the funeral home. Adults expect children to go through crises acting as if they were adults. Of course, this is not a fair judg-ment of what the child is experiencing.

The pastor must realize that, for most children, childhood is not ideal but is filled with stresses and strains, doubts and fears, losses and separations, traumas and nightmares, because chil-dren also go through death, divorce, geographical moves, mo-lestation, disease, illness, and accident. As pastors learn the "language" of childhood they will know more about how children are responding to and communicating about these experiences.

CHILDREN'S AWARENESS

Since children communicate differently from adults and have shorter attention spans, it is common for adults to assume the children do not know what is occurring in the family. Because their play activity might be punctuated by laughter, shouting, and other signs of fun and merrymaking, adults may suppose the children are unaware of the seriousness of what is happening. Some will even draw the false conclusion that the children do not care.

Children, however, are not insensitive to most events that take place in their world. They know when something is bothering their parents or siblings. They overhear telephone conversations, notice the difference in tone of voice, feel tension in the air, and sense the hurt or fear in those close to them. They do not know exactly what to do about it, so they cope in ways we can misunderstand. In summary, we will be closer to the truth if we assume children *do* know what is going on.

CHILDREN'S ADAPTABILITY

Closely related to the romanticized image of childhood is the mistaken idea that children are so adaptable that they do not have any crises until the teen years. Even when we realize that children know what is happening, we may benignly assume that their hurts, fears, and stresses are transitory. "Get a good night's sleep and things will be better in the morning" and "Tomorrow they won't even remember" are phrases that go unexamined and allow us to ignore or minimize the child's stresses and anxieties.

It is true that children are adaptable. They learn quickly and change their perceptions more easily than adults. This adaptability, however, is also a vulnerability. Because children think very concretely, they can easily distort events and misinterpret the meanings of a crisis. Their unexpressed and unexamined conclusions about what caused the crisis, what the results will be, and what role they played in it may have a destructive impact that will last a lifetime.

This same adaptability, of course, makes children prime candidates for crisis intervention. As one of my colleagues put it, this is one reason why orthodontists and child therapists like working with children. Children are growing and developing so rapidly that channeling the process of maturation is relatively easy. Intervening in a child's crisis gives the pastor an opportunity to direct creatively the child's pilgrimage toward personal and spiritual maturity.

CHILDREN AS THEIR PARENTS' RESPONSIBILITY

Another reason why children are neglected by the pastor is the long-standing cultural value that it is the parents who are responsible for taking care of their children, meeting their needs, giving advice, and providing for their spiritual nurture. Not too long ago a typical response of parents to anyone trying to help their children might have been, "No outsider knows my kids better than me, nor tells me how to raise them!" Until fairly recent times, what parents did or didn't do with their children was the parents' business ("a family matter") regardless of how much it differed from community morality. Legal protection for the child through humanitarian laws that uphold children's rights is fairly new.

The pastor may be quite hesitant to offer pastoral care to a child for fear that the parents would perceive this to be an intrusion into "family affairs." Children can unwittingly reveal more about the family than parents want exposed, and the pastor may try to avoid this risk by avoiding the children. Actually, if children do reveal something problematic about the family, it provides the pastor with an opportunity to initiate pastoral care with the larger family. I hope pastors will take the risk.

Some parents, particularly those who are not in your parish, or who do not know you or do not like you, may be resentful of your involvement with their children. Most parents are concerned, however, that their children develop into well-

rounded persons, including their spiritual life and faith com-
mitments. They realize that informed, compassionate pastoral
involvement with children can contribute to this goal. As your
parishioners come to respect and trust you they will trust your
work with their children. If you have any doubts, talk with
parents about your interest, objectives, and methods so that
any threat to them can be reduced.

AVOIDING SUSPICION

Several pastors have mentioned that their concern for avoiding suspicion has curtailed their involvement with children. In
this day and time, when so much information about child mo-
lestation and abuse has been distributed and public sensitivity
about the misuse of children is so high, it does make us all more
self-conscious about our relationships with children. While the
increased awareness about child abuse is basically good (and
we should be in the forefront as educators for children's
rights), it can have a negative effect if it creates barriers between children and adults. We must push for the former and
resist the latter.

The best way to overcome this fear is to make it a clear
agenda with the church and with the families why and how you
want to offer pastoral care to children. We will return to this
theme in chapter 4 with specific suggestions.

CHILDREN AS NONCONTRIBUTORS

It might be hard for you to imagine that your motives for
pastoral care could be influenced by the parishioner's potential
for helping the church and contributing to your ministry, but
at least allow this question to run through your mind: "Could
it be that I do not give pastoral care to children because they
don't return the favor?" After all, we need contributors and
producers if the church is to prosper (or in some cases survive),
but children do not give money, provide leadership, teach
church school, or serve on committees. They produce neither
statistics nor cash. To get even more personal, children do not
praise your sermons, affirm your leadership, or give thanks for

your attentiveness. Ministry to adults may seem more necessary in the light of what you need from them.

I must point out that in some evangelical denominations,
where "making a profession of faith" is basic to the practical
theology of the people and a goal for ministry to children,
children can be contributors in the sense that "winning" them
is perceived to be an important pastoral task. Ideally, this responsibility leads the pastor to relate creatively with children
as one aspect of nurturing children's spiritual development. It
can be negative, however, when the task is seen as simply
gaining verbal assent to some propositional statements. Then
the child's contribution as a statistic may become the major
motivation behind pastoral involvement. Child evangelism
must meet the child's needs, not the pastor's.

CHILD CARE STEREOTYPED AS WOMAN'S WORK

Most pastors are male, yet they do not receive from society
the same level of confirmation and affirmation of their masculine identity that is available to other men. Pastors often feel
neutered or demasculinized. They may work hard at establishing masculine credentials through activity defined in our society as masculine, for example, building, being in male groups,
functioning aggressively, being the authority (boss), and so
forth. Furthermore, the pastor often works extensively with
women who do much of the volunteer work at the church
anyway. So what about the children? The pastor is likely to feel
inside himself, My goodness, that is woman's work and one
thing I can get the women to do.

A friend of mine, the pastor of a small-town church, told me
a personal story that illustrates this stereotype at work. The
week prior to our conversation about this issue had been Holy
Week. On Saturday the Sunday school workers of his church
put on an Easter egg hunt for the children. My friend was busy
helping hide the eggs when it suddenly dawned on him that
only he and the women were performing this task. All the men
were gathered over by the pickup trucks talking about crops,
sports, and politics. He was immediately aware of "feeling
unmanly" and "being embarrassed at doing what the women

were doing." He reported how strongly tempted he was to drop what he was doing and join the men. He was able to continue hiding eggs only after a conscious internal struggle about the nature of his masculinity and his intention to resist stereotyped sex roles.

In short, the male pastor who is struggling to establish within himself a sense of personal strength that includes the idea that "I am a man even though I am a preacher/clergyman and interested in spiritual (feminine?) things" will find it difficult to care for children because of his bondage to cultural stereotypes. Conversely, a male pastor will be able to give consistent, sustained pastoral care to children to the degree that he has established a strong personal identity as a male.

The female pastor may also find her ministry to children hampered by the "caring for children is woman's work" stereotype. She may have expended much energy in her professional preparation for ministry trying to escape the inevitable "but you're a woman, how can you be a pastor?" hassle. She may feel that caring for children now will expose her to perceptions that she was, after all, "destined to be a mother" (if she wasn't actually a mother already) or functions best in a traditional woman's role. Working with children may seem somehow demeaning or regressive. If she feels herself identified as the minister involved in children's work, she may fear some deemphasis of her interest in the other pastoral functions. The female pastor therefore has to gain a clear sense of pastoral purpose, and come to a personally satisfying perception of herself as woman *and* pastor, before she can feel comfortable giving pastoral care to children.

THE PASTOR'S LACK OF TRAINING

Few pastors are trained to care for children. Professional education in seminaries and divinity schools rarely includes a course on the pastoral care of children. At best, the pastor may have had two weeks given to this area in an introductory course on pastoral ministry.

Advanced courses in pastoral care and counseling (pastoral ministry, pastoral psychology, pastoral theology) do include studies in theories of personality development, which are important for understanding children. These theories, however, are usually applied to understanding and counseling adults who are in trouble, rather than children. These advanced courses also include study of counseling techniques and different methods of psychotherapeutic intervention. But not much attention is given to counseling techniques, or to just plain interactional skills, which are effective with children.

A few pastors elect a course in the Christian education department designed to help ministers understand children. However, these courses do not usually pursue either the uniqueness of the pastor's role with children or the care of children in crisis. In short, as a student at a seminary or divinity school you would not get the idea that the pastoral care of children was an important task, much less receive any specific training in the pastoral care of children in crisis.

THE PASTOR'S SENSE OF INADEQUACY

Most of us choose to avoid situations that make us feel inadequate. Caring for children seems to be a mine field of uncertainties. Pastors excuse themselves from pastoral care of children because they don't know much about them, don't feel confident or competent relating to children, and are afraid of making a mistake. Why the uncertainties, fears, and concerns? Some are rooted in the apparent differences between caring for adults and caring for children.

A good pastor, for example, wants to be effective in pastoral care. When we care for adults we have some basic goals and objectives for our ministry, which means there are some rough criteria that help us know when we have been effective. With children, however, the pastor does not know what goals and objectives to adopt, which means that there are no criteria providing checks on whether or not the pastor's interaction has been helpful and meaningful or boring and ineffective. This leaves the pastor, who needs feedback about ministry in order to feel adequate, in limbo. Learning to set goals for ministry with children becomes important if the pastor is to feel comfortable in such ministry.

Closely related is our uncertainty as pastors about how we are being perceived by children. We are not sure if the child understands who we are, what we do, why we are visiting, or what we want "to do" with them. Adults, for better or worse, have established their ideas about us and have some background which enables them to understand our role and function. We can either confirm or try to reconstruct their perceptions. Caring for children, however, puts more of a burden on us to communicate our identity, role, and function with concepts and actions understandable to children. I hope this book will show that such a task is not as difficult as it seems.

Communication methods are also an uncertainty. How do you talk with children? What do you say after you ask them about school? We use regular communication skills and normal vocabulary with adults, but with children it is easy to become self-conscious about the whole process. Some pastors talk louder (as if the child were deaf) and slower (as if the child were retarded). Which words are too big? we wonder, as we censor our speech for things the child would not understand.

Even the pastors who are sensitive to the needs and hurts of children (and I have met many) are hindered by their lack of training. They want to be involved, but their self-consciousness in interactions with children is anxiety producing. It is easy to shy away from situations in which we feel so vulnerable.

For all these reasons, many pastors avoid children. The result of this neglect is that children are left without effective pastoral care. We have been unfaithful to them as shepherds. If we are to be different, we must change our perceptions of our responsibility for children.

2

CHILDREN ARE
PARISHIONERS TOO!

The lone shepherd in the ancient lands of Judea and Galilee, guarding his flock by night, leading them to pasture and water by day, binding up the wounds of the injured sheep, and seeking the lambs when they are lost, may not seem like a relevant model for pastoral care in urban/suburban North America. From my perspective, however, the shepherd is still a valid model, not because the specific tasks are the same, but because the functions of guarding, guiding, nurturing, healing, and seeking are still the major functions of the faithful pastor.[1]

If you accept the shepherding model, pursue with me this question, "Was there an age limit on the sheep who were cared for by the shepherd?" Of course not. The youngest lamb was also the recipient of the shepherd's guarding, guiding, nurturing, healing, and seeking. In fact, since the young lambs were the most defenseless, and because they represented the future, they probably received a disproportionate amount of the shepherd's attention.

In today's church some of these pastoral functions are pursued through the Christian education program and by including children in worship. Some larger churches employ people to direct a complete children's program. However, when examining the amount of time and energy expended by pastors in caring for children, we find that today's pastoral shepherds are more likely to ignore the needs of the younger members of the flock. I wonder, do we perceive children to *be* parishioners or to *belong to* parishioners? When the Johnson family is leaving after the service and you lean over to pat Bobby on the head and routinely note, "Doesn't Sally look pretty today?" is that any different from when you compliment their new car or ask how the tomato plants are doing?

We must be reminded that children are parishioners too. And therefore they have a right to be recipients of our pastoral care. We have the responsibility to be intentional in our pastoral care of children by taking seriously their unique needs and experiences. They deserve our time, our energy, and our helping skills. I offer the following reasons why shepherding children should be included in the shepherding task.

JESUS AND CHILDREN

Jesus serves, for most of us, as a model for mature faith in action and, more specifically, for faithful, effective ministry. Therefore we must learn what value he placed on children and where they fit in his ministry priorities. We can do this by examining his encounters with children.[2]

Jesus' Identification with Children

When the disciples were arguing over "who was the greatest" (Mark 9:34), Jesus took the opportunity to acquaint them with the ideas of humility and service (9:35). He did so by discussing the importance of relating to children.

> And he took a child, and put him in the midst of them; and taking him in his arms, he said to them, "Whoever receives one such child in my name receives me; and whoever receives me, receives not me but him who sent me." (Mark 9:36–37)

Jesus so identifies himself with the children that he can tell those who care for children that they have in effect cared for him. Those who love as Jesus loved will love children. To receive (care for, accept) children is to care for, accept, and make room in our hearts for Jesus and also for the one who sent him—God. Because children are so important to God, caring for children is one way to come into the presence of God. To minister to children is to hear, "Well done, good and faithful servant."

Jesus' Anger

One of the most well known events in Scripture describes Jesus' confrontation of the disciples for keeping the children away from him.

> And they were bringing children to him, that he might touch them; and the disciples rebuked them. But when Jesus saw it he was indignant, and said to them, "Let the children come to me, do not hinder them; for to such belongs the kingdom of God." (Mark 10:13–14)

It was a custom among the Jews to bring their children to holy men, priests and rabbis, to be blessed. So it was that some people (parents probably) were wanting Jesus to bless (lay hands on and pray for, Matt. 19:13) their children (even infants, Luke 18:15). For some reason, the disciples were upset by the situation. Perhaps they were protecting their Master's time or concerned about his lack of rest. They may have decided that other ministries, such as healing and teaching, were more important than blessing the children. Maybe they thought the children were insignificant. In any case, they began to rebuke the parents, trying to keep the children away from Jesus.

The disciples failed to consult with Jesus about their perceptions and attempted to act on his behalf. When he became aware of their stance, he became "indignant." The Greek word is a highly intense word and conveys the fact that Jesus was emotionally charged, angry that the disciples would so misunderstand who he was and what he was about.

Jesus' Warning

Jesus' identification with and commitment to children, plus his anger toward anyone who would keep children from him, is confirmed in his warning to those who get in the way of a child's belief.

> Whoever causes one of these little ones who believe in me to sin, it would be better for him if a great millstone were hung round his neck and he were thrown into the sea. (Mark 9:42)

Jesus seems to refer to the natural ability of children to trust the creation, and by implication the Creator, unless distorted by adults. We know that the learning of mistrust and the loss of "faith" can begin early if the parenting and nurturing figures in a child's life are not trustworthy in their care. We know that traumas, accidents, and abuse at any time during childhood can lead to fear and mistrust.

Pastoral care of children would include being present to help children sort out life events that raise questions about the reliability of creation. Our involvement might help them decide to keep on trusting. To neglect them in their time of need is to be guilty by omission of allowing them to stumble into unbelief.

Jesus' Invitation

After Jesus expressed his dissatisfaction, he ordered the disciples to make way for the children.

> Let the children come to me, do not hinder them; for to such belongs the kingdom of God. (Mark 10:14)

He invited the children to spend time with him, to be around him, to talk with him. Can you envision their response to his smile, their careful answers to his gentle questions, their enjoyment of his obvious pleasure in their company, their appreciation for his advocacy on their behalf? Children were obviously important to Jesus, perhaps even refreshing to him in their simple faith. After all, he was on his way to Jerusalem and the cross.

Few pastors would intentionally inhibit children from "coming to Jesus." The question is whether we actively, purposefully, work to bring them into his presence. If we are not careful, we will hide Jesus from the children with rituals, symbols, and sermons that are beyond their ability to comprehend. At our best, we will try to interpret our faith, including our rituals and symbols, in words and deeds they can understand. After all, a primary goal of pastoral care is to provide a context, an atmosphere, in which an individual can meet God.

It is easy for the pastor to assume that providing this opportunity is the work of the Christian education program, or that it is taken care of during the children's worship period on Sunday morning. Both of these, of course, are immeasurably important, but they do not take the place of faithful pastoral care from Monday morning through Saturday night when the children are grappling with all that life can throw at them. We can be most faithful if we take advantage of every opportunity, particularly during crises, to "bring" children to Jesus.

Jesus' Touch

When Jesus was with children he felt free to touch them.

> And he took a child, and put him in the midst of them; and taking him in his arms . . . (Mark 9:36)

> And he took them in his arms and blessed them, laying his hands upon them. (Mark 10:16)

We know how important touch is to infants.[3] Touch is their major contact with people and the first way they can feel loved (or unloved!). Through touch they become connected with others and aware of human relationships. During childhood, touch continues to be a meaningful way of communicating love, interest, joy, and acceptance. As a pastor, you convey the same message that Jesus conveyed when you take time to get at eye level with children by picking them up, or stooping and placing them on your knee, or, when sitting, inviting them to your lap. A hand on the shoulder, a pat on the back (not the head!), holding hands, or even a handshake can solidify your relationship with a child.

Touch is, of course, usually more meaningful when the relationship is under way and rapport with the child is already established. Touching before the child knows you may be uncomfortable to the child and the parents. Children have a sense of personal territory, just as adults, and must give you permission to enter. Watch the child's body language to know whether touch is acceptable. As the child grows older you will have to alter your method of touch.

Do you ever imagine yourself holding children? Certainly *1985* you have mental pictures of what it means to be a good pastor: diligently studying the word of God in your study, faithfully standing by the bedside of the sick, persuasively preaching the Word from the pulpit, and being courageously prophetic in the face of social injustice. I wish you would add to this the image of holding the children in your arms and blessing them. Can you imagine the impact on a child who, having been gently lifted into your arms in the vestibule, hears you whisper in his ear, "I love you and God loves you too"!

Jesus' Blessing

An almost totally forgotten aspect of pastoral care is the pastoral blessing.[4] Jesus knew it could be meaningful to children (and to their parents). Nowadays this happens only at baptisms and dedications.

> And he took them in his arms and blessed them, laying his hands upon them. (Mark 10:16)

What did the blessing represent? What did it mean? Certainly it communicates to the children that they are special in the sight of those who know God. It makes God's love concrete to the child who sings in Sunday school,

> Jesus loves the little children,
> All the children of the world.
> Red and yellow, black and white,
> All are precious in his sight.
> Jesus loves the little children of the world.

THE FAMILY OF GOD

Elsewhere in the New Testament, we believers in Jesus, the Christ, learn to think about ourselves as a family, God's family.

> I will be a father to you, and you shall be my sons and daughters, says the Lord Almighty. (2 Cor. 6:18)

> You have received the spirit of sonship. When we cry,
> "Abba! Father!" it is the Spirit himself bearing witness
> with our spirit that we are children of God. (Rom. 8:
> 15–16)

Yes, we regard the church as the family of God and ourselves as brothers and sisters in Christ. In most denominations, children are included in this family through either baptism or dedication. And if a family's concern is not for its children, whom is it for?

We expect families to provide food, clothing, shelter, and security for their children. Furthermore, we expect these families to pass on their values and their faith. The church works at "passing on the faith" through its educational program and in worship. Yet we continue to wonder what will happen to our children. Will we be able to pass on to them the faith of our fathers and mothers? In an age when secularism is so dominant and much of the religion that gains public exposure is so immature, or magical, or even pathological, how will our children find a meaningful Christian faith?[5] Another way we can pass on our faith is by helping children perceive the spiritual dimensions of their crises. If God's presence can be experienced in crisis, the spiritual dimension of life becomes more open, more possible, more real, and more desirable to the child. This is primarily a task for the pastor.

At their best, families will also care for their children when they are stressed or struggling. In our churches, however, children who are in crises may not be receiving the level of pastoral care that adults have historically expected from their pastor. At this point we are failing those for whom the family of God has the most responsibility.

When Wayne Oates wrote to parents and teachers about children, he chose to name this timeless little book *On Becoming Children of God.* The title is taken from the words in the Fourth Gospel which announce, "To all who received him, who believed in his name, he gave power to become children of God" (John 1:12).

Oates points out that his title could be challenged by those who would question whether we *become* children of God. They rather claim that we *are* children of God. Oates agrees, of course, that in one sense, "We are made in his likeness. He has made us for himself."[6] But he goes on to ask further questions. "We know we are created in God's image. But *when* is that creation an accomplished fact? at conception? at birth? at 'the age of accountability'? Or is that creation ever finished short of the resurrection?"[7] Then he describes the tension between our completeness and incompleteness as children of God. We both *are* and are *becoming,* since "creation continues in the course and process of human life."[8]

The family of God has the responsibility of monitoring this process of "becoming" so that it may affect the outcome in every possible way. The pastor, as shepherd of this flock, must be particularly aware of his or her role in helping the children become "faithing" persons, individuals on pilgrimage. We cannot sit passively and hope they turn out okay. We must be actively involved, knowing that our pastoral care could provide significant reference points for the little ones as they are becoming children of God.

Before leaving this subject, we must point out that our claim *to be* "children of God," and to include children in that category, suggests another reason why pastoral care to children is imperative. Those of us in the pastoral care field have always been committed to a strong belief in the value of personhood. We respect the uniqueness of each individual. We can do no less for children. They too have worth and value as persons in the sight of God. They too deserve recognition and response from the pastor just because they *are.*

THE INCARNATION

Perhaps the strongest imperative for giving pastoral care to children is our conviction that God was in Christ, being revealed in new and profound ways as the God-who-is-Love and who wants to be known by and reconciled with all people. And, in an amazing contradiction of expectation, God chose to become known by taking on the form of a child. God chose in Jesus Christ to take on humanness in order, among other things, to be made known to us. This incarnational theology underlies and motivates most pastoral care, because we are convinced that the Christian gospel is still communicated most completely through human beings.[9] And what is this gospel we proclaim? That this God we worship, who is the creator and sustainer of the universe, is a God-who-is-Love and that this love is expressed toward us through God's grace, trustworthiness, acceptance, and forgiveness.

Because of our unique identity as pastors, and our role as shepherds of the flock, representatives of God, symbols of our religious quest, and students of spirituality, we have a unique opportunity to incarnate the gospel to children in ways no one else can do. Through our personhood, which includes these images, we can proclaim the God we worship in ways that children will never forget.

How Children View the Pastor

Have you ever wondered what the children in your church think about you? Benjamin Griffin, when pastor in York, Pennsylvania, did some original research with 109 children, ages three to twelve, in church school classes at six different churches.[10] He asked them two simple questions: "Who is the pastor (minister, preacher)?" and "What does he do?" The responses were humorous but revealing.

The pastor was associated in the children's minds with God and the church:

"I think he's the man who lives in the church."
"God, I think."
"He runs the church."
"He talks about God and being good. Things like that."

They also described him as doing religious acts:

"He preaches and prays."
"Oh, I know. He marries people."
"Does something when babies are brought to church—puts water on their head."

And, quite important, they identified the pastor with crises:

"Talks when someone dies."
"He sees people in the hospital when they are sick."
"He came to see us when Pop-Pop died."
"He helps people."
"Rev. _____ came to see me in the hospital."

Many children, says Griffin, communicated "an aura of mystery or magic about the pastor and sometimes fear."[11] Usually the children had no personal relationship with the pastor, who was seen as a distant figure. Yet the ways in which the pastor was described, plus the events and acts with which he was associated, point out the potential significance the pastor could have in the life of a child. Griffin points out, "The fact that children often associated the pastor with symbolic (perhaps magical) meaning can be used, if used properly, in the minister's pastoral care."[12]

All pastors are aware of the symbolic meaning expressed through their office and/or their personhood, depending on the emphasis within their particular denominational heritage. "The clergy[person] is a physical representation of the whole community of faith, of the tradition, of a way of viewing the meaning of life, of the dynamic power of faith, and of God."[13] Pastoral care literature has focused on this representational aspect of the pastoral role but seldom points out that it can be even more true for children than for adults. The child's perceptions of the pastor, which set the stage for the symbolic meanings, are shaped by (1) what they have heard and interpreted (both thought and feeling) from their parents, other adults, and peers, (2) their own experiences with the pastor, and (3) what they fantasize from the first two.

One of the exciting opportunities with children is that, because their perception of what you symbolize is not yet poured in concrete (as it is with many adults), your pastoral care of them can correct perceptions of pastors and all that pastors represent. How you relate to children may well affect how they view the church and God throughout the rest of their lives. Can such an opportunity be ignored, even if it does create anxiety?

Your ultimate uniqueness is in your symbolic power as a representative of God and the community of faith.[14] No matter how much you know about personality development and child psychology (and I hope you learn as much as you can), and regardless of how skilled you are in counseling (and I hope you're good), the unique thing you have to offer children in crisis is your religious commitment and your role as a representative of God. This fact may make you uncomfortable, even cause you to shy away from involvement with children. I hope, however, that you will come to see it as a challenge and take the risk of relating to children both "because of" and "through" your special uniqueness as their pastor. Note briefly some aspects of God's love which can be transmitted, or incarnated, through your pastoral ministry to children.

Trust

We believe that God is trustworthy. We have experienced God's faithfulness. Our tradition has counted on God's steadfast love. From those who study personality development, we learn that the development of trust is a crucial ingredient in the first two years of life and continues to be a basic component of love. Children learn to trust when those who care for them are trustworthy.

We want our children to develop trust in God, which means they must experience God as trustworthy. But how can they experience God as trustworthy, faithful, steadfast? Through parents and other significant adults in the parish, to be sure, but also by experiencing the designated representative of God (the one who conveys the Word, leads worship, and prays on behalf of the church) as one who is faithful and steadfast.

How can the pastor communicate through his or her personhood that God is trustworthy? Children learn to trust those who are trustworthy in their faithfulness. One way they measure faithfulness is by presence. When the pastor takes time to be with them, children can imagine that God is interested in them also.

Children develop trust when they perceive that the significant adults in their lives enjoy being around them and seem glad to have children around. When Jesus invited the children

("Let the children come to me") and blessed them and prayed with them, he was certainly conveying that he loved them. I imagine that when he gave permission for them to approach, they must have flocked around him, basking in his enjoyment of them. Jesus comments on their trust when he says, "Truly, I say to you, whoever does not receive the kingdom of God like a child shall not enter it" (Mark 10:15).

Forgiveness

Do our children feel guilty? Yes, they are able to feel responsible for parents divorcing, pets dying, and siblings having accidents. Is it real guilt? Probably not, and it is appropriate to try to help the child see that he or she did not cause these events. But can children accomplish that totally, while in childhood? Probably not, but they can begin to understand that God forgives, understands, has mercy upon us, and loves us "anyway." This forgiveness can be conveyed by the pastor, who accepts and understands and forgives. Also, God's forgiveness can be conveyed indirectly through pastoral conversation, as we shall discuss later.

Prayer

We believe in a God who listens, who wants to know our needs, who desires communication with the crown of creation. Our God is interested in knowing what we think and feel. And how can we introduce this fact to children? By modeling God's interest through our investment in communicating *with* them. Not just talking *to* them, but listening—listening so carefully that we can discern their real needs and concerns and questions. Then, when we respond accurately, they can begin to get the message that God listens and responds also. Believing (and experiencing) that God cares, and is both able and willing to participate in our lives, is the first step in developing a life-style that includes prayer and meditation.

CHILDREN'S CRISES

Finally, we offer pastoral care to children because life is not a rose garden for them either. Our romanticized view of childhood, plus our general lack of attention to their life situations, leads us to overlook that they have crises.[15] After talking with one group of pastors about children's crises, I asked them to describe the children in their parish who were in crisis that week. They were surprised to come up with the following: an eight-year-old girl had been sexually molested by a neighbor; a nine-year-old boy's grandfather, who lived with the boy's family, died yesterday in the home; a mother of two girls, nine and eleven, was hospitalized for the fifth time with breast cancer and was not expected to return home; a twelve-year-old boy had broken both arms in a weight-lifting accident; and they knew a number of children whose parents had been divorced within the last six months.

It would be the same in your church. When sensitized to the types of stress and anxiety that children can experience, you will realize that in any given week there are children in your church who need pastoral care. At the time of this writing comes news of the death of over seventy persons from tornadoes in North and South Carolina. Over five hundred were injured and the damage was extensive. Think how many children were affected by these disasters. Will they receive pastoral care? Will the pastors be aware that the surviving children are in crisis? Will the pastors take seriously the grief, loneliness, fear, guilt, shame, failure, despair, anger, hurt, and so forth, that will plague the surviving children as well as the adults? From a Christian perspective, to ignore these children would be to sin against them.

It is of critical importance to intervene in children's crises, because how they experience and interpret the crisis will affect every part of their developing selfhood. Daniel Day Williams, in his book *The Minister and the Care of Souls,* describes "the principles of linkage in human experience." He says that "God's creature is the being who finds . . . that every part of his being and experience is linked actually or potentially with every other part."[16] Intervening in children's crises, enabling them to cope effectively with both the internal and the external turmoil, allows each child to integrate the critical experience into a developing "sense of self," as Gordon Allport called it.[17] When children "work through" a crisis and handle it effectively, their sense of self-worth is enhanced and they are better prepared for effective coping with future crises. They gain competence, and the resulting confidence that they can master what is "thrown" at them.

When children do not receive pastoral care during a stressful event, the meaning of the crisis may be distorted, the emotions suppressed, and the impact denied. Many times, faulty conclusions are reached about the nature of God and God's way of relating to the world. Without careful pastoral guidance, the child may decide that God is angry, or uncaring, or mean. Without help, the unresolved and distorted aspects of the crisis may continue to plague the child throughout the childhood years and into adolescence, or return as haunting "demons" in their adult years.

We know that many of the emotional, relational, and spiritual problems with which adults suffer result from childhood crises that were not resolved creatively. Effective pastoral care with a child in crisis may prevent the crisis from having a lifelong debilitating effect on the child's emotional, physical, and spiritual health.

We know, for example, that the way separation and loss are experienced and coped with during childhood sets the precedent for how separation and loss is handled in adulthood. Those who stifle grief, with its attendant fear, anger, and depression, in childhood will tend to suppress these emotions as adults. This makes it difficult to be mature during adult crises.

Pastoral care with children in crisis can enable them to make theological sense, in a childlike way, out of both the external events and their internal responses. They can learn to interpret the crisis and its resolution in spiritual terms. In his classic book *The Christian Pastor,* Wayne Oates builds on this principle and underscores the crucial possibility of pastoral care to children in crisis when he writes:

> Human crises are not *necessarily* but only potentially bearers of the mystery of the eternal God. The meaningful personal participation of the individual and the group in a decisive and responsible commitment to God through

faith turns a potentially religious crisis into an actual one. The "shaping environment" of the community of faith and its ministers—official or not—makes the difference.[18]

The Christian pastor has always been expected to be present as God's representative in times of stress, with the anticipation that in this role he or she can help people make spiritual sense out of the chaos of a crisis. Children have a right to this same act of ministry.

To minister effectively to children in crisis we must know just how a crisis affects a child's growing sense of self, including his or her attitudes, values, perceptions, feelings, and religious faith. Such knowledge is based on understanding the major patterns of psychosocial growth and development that occurs during these childhood years. We turn our attention to this task.

3

WHAT CHILDREN IN CRISIS NEED FROM THE PASTOR

As a seasoned pastor you realize that the more you know and understand about people, the more focused and effective will be your care of them. It is no different with children. Since you not only want to be *faithful* in your care of children but also want to be *effective,* it is important to learn as much as possible about them. It is a blessing that a variety of specialists from the social and behavioral sciences[19] have learned so much about children.

It is not necessary for you to know all the technical data that enable these professionals to help children who have serious physical, social, or emotional difficulties. It is important, however, to know the process of social and psychological development that occurs during this stage in life. Understanding what children are thinking, feeling, perceiving, deciding, and experiencing during the preadolescent years will enrich your relationships with them.[20] Remember, this chapter and the remainder of the book are focused specifically on preadolescents, children between five and twelve years of age (school-age children).

During this stage in life, children need both to experience some things from others and to accomplish some things for themselves. This process can be either interrupted or enhanced by crises. You have much to offer the children in your parish, and they need many things that you can choose to give. In what follows we (1) describe some of the most basic needs, (2) discuss the impact of crises on these needs, and (3) prescribe some rules of thumb for pastoral care.

A SENSE OF COMPETENCE

Accomplishing certain tasks, such as walking, talking, feeding oneself, controlling bowel and bladder functions, and making toys work, is necessary to completing early childhood and preparing for the school-age years. Satisfactory accomplishment of these tasks results, usually, in receiving affirmation from parents and other significant adults. Their encouragement, excitement, and obvious pleasure establish the early sense of satisfaction and accomplishment experienced by the child. Children who do not receive positive feedback, of course, may not have this early sense of worth and may already be doubtful of their ability. Until kindergarten, children are barely aware of comparing themselves with others, but as they enter formal schooling such comparisons are inevitable. Children who have used parental standards and vague internal criteria for success now face pressure from teachers and peers to learn certain things and perform certain tasks.

The peer group, for example, now functions in a more organized manner around physical activities that involve running, jumping, climbing, swimming, tumbling, and throwing, kicking, hitting, or catching a ball—all of which demand both large muscle and eye and hand coordination. Children, both boys and girls, who cannot function adequately in these activities may be subject to teasing and ridicule. Such loss of approval is hard on self-esteem. When children are taught these activities and have time to practice so they gain some proficiency, their sense of competency is greatly enhanced.

Adults may think that physical appearance is not important until adolescence. Not so. Elementary school children compare themselves both to peers and to cultural norms. Those who are too tall, or short, or fat, or whose looks do not measure up, will feel self-conscious and may feel inferior.

Intellectual development gains momentum during this stage in life. Cognitive ability expands and changes rapidly, making it possible to read, write, and think logically and mathematically. While children who acquire this new knowledge and learn the skills find their sense of competence enhanced, those who falter will bog down in a sense of inferiority. These children who do not gain the all-important competencies may withdraw, or compensate by acting in ways that are problematic for both the school and the family.

This task of developing competence is so important that Erik Erikson has made it central to his theory of psychosocial development for this age group. He calls it the stage of "industry vs. inferiority."[21] Both at school and at play, children are exploring their new physical, social, and intellectual potential and testing themselves against the expectations of both peers and adults. Approval from others, and from within themselves, leads to a sense of worth rooted in the sense of mastery. The children who succeed come to believe that if they apply themselves to a new task, they will probably learn it or accomplish it. Those who fail or meet with disapproval move in the opposite direction. They become fearful of new tasks, for fear of further failure, and avoid new opportunities because of their sense of inferiority and inadequacy.

The church can help children develop a sense of competency through varied programs, but I wish to focus on our subject of pastoral care in crisis. When a crisis occurs, particularly for children, competency is challenged. In the face of a disease, a hospital visit, a death in the family, an accident, or a trauma, the children (like most adults) will probably feel out of control, the victims of circumstances, unprepared, confused and helpless. It is easy for adults to shunt children aside when crises occur. If significant adults leave the child out of the "dealing with" the crisis, however, then the child's perception of his or her inadequacy in the face of the crisis is confirmed and contributes to a sense of inferiority.

When children are included in the process of confronting and responding to the challenge posed by the crisis, then their sense of competence is greatly enhanced. They feel that their abilities are recognized and trusted by the adults. When they offer real help (as they almost always will) in solving, decision-making, reconciling, accepting, and otherwise dealing with the crisis, they gain an immeasurable sense of mastery, of being able to handle what life throws at them, which is so important for their sense of competence and self-esteem. You, as the pastor, can make sure that children are included rather than excluded in what the family is up against, particularly when the crisis focuses on the child.

ATTITUDES AND VALUES

When children enter kindergarten, early impressions about many things have been established. The child has not, however, had the cognitive ability or the experience to form many attitudes toward the vast world external to the family. During the childhood years upon which we are focusing, children are in the process of developing and conceptualizing their attitudes toward major aspects in both their local social environment and the wider culture, such as education, money, ethnic groups, sex, sports, work, television, family styles, church and religion, and, we would add, crises such as illness, grief, death, and divorce. When entering kindergarten, children are limited in what they know about any of these aspects of their society.

> Yet, by the end of elementary school, this same child has a full complement of social attitudes, picked up or absorbed from his [her] family, his [her] teachers, his [her] peer groups, and his [her] contact with the community and the wider world through movies, radio, television, books, and lectures.[22]

We know from psychological and sociological studies that these social attitudes are internalized and become the norm for children throughout life unless challenged and changed by significant new experience or learning.

For those of us interested in the child's religious and spiritual growth, it is imperative that we help give shape to these evolving attitudes, because they set the foundation for the child's later belief system. These developing attitudes, for example, will include the value systems that are so integral to the child's future ethical stance. Since we want our children to grow into adults who are committed to a Christian ethic, we must influence their evolving attitudes and belief systems during these crucial years. Christian parents (and you, the reader, may be one) and church school teachers are primarily involved in this process, but pastors can choose to be an integral part.

Robert Havighurst, the famous developmental psychologist, suggests that children learn attitudes in three basic ways: (1) by imitating the attitudes of persons whom the child admires and respects, (2) through a collection of experience (either pleasant or unpleasant) with a given idea, group, or institution and their memories and perceptions of these encounters, and (3) through a single, intense, deeply emotional experience (either pleasant or unpleasant) with some object, person, or situation.[23]

With these three ideas in mind, you will not have to stretch your imagination very far to recognize how much impact you and your pastoral care to children can contribute to their developing ideas about religious and spiritual matters. If they experience you as a kind, gentle, interested, genuine pastor whom they learn to respect and admire, then they will want to imitate, as Havighurst says, your attitudes and values. Attitudes that you express, not only in your children's sermons, special classes, and retreats but also in your marketplace conversation with children, are tucked away in the back pockets of their minds as being accurate and valid because of who you are. Not only your words, of course, but your actions too will be noticed and copied. How you relate to people of different ages, nationalities, socioeconomic positions, and gender will set the example they will adopt if you have become a person they admire.

Perhaps most important to our purpose is Havighurst's third point, that attitudes are formed by a single, intense, deeply emotional experience with some object, person, or situation. Crises are such intense, emotional experiences. How we care for children during their critical encounters with death, divorce, illness, accident, and other traumas may well influence the development of healthy Christian attitudes and values about life's slings and arrows. Furthermore, since you are God's representative, and children perceive you that way, they will not only imitate your values but develop the concept of living out God's purposes. In fact, many people's concepts of what God is like, how God works in the world, and how God feels about them are formed during childhood crises. Something as simple as a pastor's prayer conveys values and attitudes which are impressed on a child.

CONFIRMATION OF THEIR PERCEPTIONS

Adults are sometimes tempted to overprotect children in a crisis by misrepresenting truth and withholding information. Children often realize that they are being deceived. When that which younger children perceive and that which they are told are not congruent, they tend to doubt themselves and their own perceptions. Children through age nine tend to think that adults are always right (even if they question adult concepts in private sessions with peers). When children doubt their own perceptions, it makes them question their competency and lowers self-esteem.

Older children also wonder about their perceptions, but they also become suspicious of the adults who are either distorting or hiding reality. Not only does self-doubt affect their sense of competency but the suspicion reduces their trust in adults—which in turn affects their sense of community.

As pastor you represent the Eternal Reality. Most Christians believe that God expects us to deal as much as possible with reality, as perceived through both our physical senses and our spiritual intuitions and experiences. To deal with distortions of reality creates problems between children and the Creator. Children, therefore, can best deal with life as it is, rather than as it may be skewed by others during a time of crisis. Like adults, children cope most courageously with what they *know.* It is what they are forced to imagine without accurate information that can be most anxiety provoking. An important prerequisite for coping adequately and creatively with a crisis is knowledge of the truth about it. Being realistic with children is one way of participating in the healing. As pastor you may be one of the few adults who will deal realistically with the child. In so doing, you represent the God who sees the world as it is, who knows the truth and responds to it. When children realize that you will deal with things as they are, it enables them to trust both you and the One you serve.

Your stance in a crisis is (1) to help the children gain accurate information, (2) to participate with them as they interpret, clarify, and respond to this data, and (3) to return to these issues in future conversations to make sure they have had ample opportunity to process and respond to their understanding of the crisis. Chapters 5 through 8 describe specific methodologies and case illustrations for providing such pastoral care.

A Sense of Belonging

In the first four years of life, the child's social development is primarily based on genetic inheritance and interactions with parents and siblings. Even in day care facilities, where children must of necessity come in contact with each other, they do not fully develop the capacity for social interaction. Their interactions with others are primarily centered around their own needs, desires, and drives—the egocentric stage.

During the grade-school years, however, children begin to shape and modify their social self, or "personality," on the basis of encounters with peers. First they begin to formulate ideas about classmates and decide how to interact accordingly. Soon they realize that just as they are making judgments about peers, these peers are forming concepts of them. Then they begin to wonder, What are they thinking about me? At this point children begin to experiment with different ways of presenting themselves and learn how to behave in ways calculated to make others draw certain conclusions—early image-making, so to speak. Mixing these intentional actions with genetic makeup and behavior traits picked up from parents, children form their social self: shy or gregarious, friendly or antagonistic, loud or quiet, assertive or passive, verbal or nonverbal, and so forth.

Before kindergarten, children play alongside rather than with anyone who happens into the same sandbox. But during elementary school, children begin to select friends on the basis of whom they feel comfortable with, whom they are like, and who gives positive feedback. With these chosen friends they learn about fair play, acceptable expressions of affection, group rules, spoken and unspoken taboos, and behavior that earns approval and makes them "fit in." Not to fit in, not to have a group, not to belong, is a terrible blow to the child's self-esteem.

Theologically speaking, we are describing the basic foundations for the ability/capacity to experience community. Children who effectively develop a social self are able to experience the fellowship (koinonia) of the church. They can become part of the body of Christ and accept the intimate possibilities and responsibilities of personal relationships. Most of the lasting friendships of this stage in life are with children of the same gender. In these close, "best friends" relationships, children are learning how to be open, trusting, and vulnerable with another person by sharing secrets and expressing affection. They are also learning about loyalty and fidelity, what it means to be committed. These lessons, for better or worse, prepare them for intimate friendships and "one flesh" marriage relationships in the future.

In a crisis the child's community is often interrupted. The need to belong may go unmet as adults, preoccupied with their own anxieties, shunt children to the side. Or, for many of the reasons we mentioned in chapter 1, adults may ignore the child's involvement in a crisis. Furthermore, the fear that children will be irreparably harmed if they have to face a crisis leads well-meaning adults to overprotect them. They do this by misrepresenting facts ("She'll be all right when they get her to the hospital"), withholding information ("We must not let the children know"), physical separation ("I want the two of you to go outside and play now," or "No, you can't go to the funeral!"), and ignoring their concerns and questions ("Not now, can't you see I'm talking to the pastor!"). As a result of this overprotection, children often feel abandoned during a crisis. They need to receive support, comfort, and reassurance, from their community. They need to be part of what is happening, because belonging is necessary in order to feel secure and loved.

Pastoral care of children in crisis must focus on the maintenance of a sense of community that includes the children. You must be an advocate of the inclusion of children in the gatherings, conversations, decisions, and debriefings of the family in crisis, even when emotionality is high. Experiencing the intensity of the family is not as threatening to children as the sense that they have been abandoned. As you insert yourself into crises, find out the whereabouts of the children. When it is appropriate, ask, "Why don't we invite the children into our discussion?" or "Let's find out what the children are thinking and feeling about going to the funeral home." When children's questions are going unanswered, use your authority to include them in the conversation: "That is a good question, Timothy, let's see who in the family can answer it." When the children experience your advocacy, it will add to their perception of you as a friend. Most important, it will relieve some of the sense of abandonment and restore their sense of belonging to a community.

ADULT FRIENDS (EVEN HEROES)

Adult friends from outside the family can play an important role in the growth and development of children. These adult friends serve as models for adult living, provide examples, set goals, and give concrete ideals for children to emulate. Parents have to discipline, which means conflict and possible resistance and resentment in the child. Adult friends outside the family carry a different type of authority and, in the case of the pastor, rarely have to get into conflict over discipline. This enables the relationship to be primarily a friendship, which makes it different from what is always possible between parent and child. Furthermore, older children usually know the dark side, the imperfect side, of their parents, perhaps becoming somewhat disillusioned. With other adult friends, children can see more of the ideal attributes and characteristics they would like to adopt for themselves. By identifying with these adult friends they strengthen their own internal images of who they want to be and become. These internal images are quite important in the formation of character. Almost every child, of course, has some ambivalence in relationship to parents, and that makes it more difficult consciously to choose them as models or heroes. To the degree that the child's relationship to his or her parents is problematic, the child needs the positive influence of an admired adult friend, such as a pastor, from outside the family.

Wayne Oates has described one basic level of pastoral care to be "the ministry of friendship," which is so important it is "the very soil of our relationships with people."[24] Oates recognizes the importance of applying this level of pastoral care to the need of children for positive adult models to admire and imitate.

> Likewise, the ministry of friendship to small children is exceptionally rewarding. Pastors give little children an example, a hero with whom to identify, and a friendship that lends security. Especially is this true in instances in which the home has been broken by death, separation, or the divorce of parents. Children of intact and happy homes need friends older than they are who are outside their family.[25]

It may seem a little strange to think of yourself as a hero to anyone, a little too close to Superman, star athletes, movie idols, and rock musicians. But school-age children need to admire and be in awe of adults who are beyond them in talent, power, or authority—adults who are in control and seem to live in the fantasy worlds about which children dream. Some of the fantasy worlds and the heroes children adopt do not exactly offer the character models Christians want for their children. How important it is that the church provide alternative heroes. More important, however, is that most of our children's heroes do not relate to them personally. If a child chooses you as a hero, you have a chance to be a hero who actually counts the child as a friend. If you remember your excitement in getting even a handshake or an autograph from your childhood heroes, you can imagine the impact you can have on children by simply letting them know that you count them among your friends. It makes children feel important when you take time to be with them, and it adds to their sense of self-worth.

On top of everything said above is the constant fact that you represent God and God's Son. When you are a model and a friend to children, they have a better chance of believing the hymn "What a Friend We Have in Jesus." When you tell them stories about Jesus' friendship with children, with Mary and Martha, and with "the beloved disciple," they will understand what and whom you represent. Blessed is the child who grows up thinking of the risen Lord as a friend.

Being in awe of an adult friend or of a distant hero is a first step in learning worship. Being worthy of such adulation is not easy, but it is important. It serves as a backbone for helping children switch their allegiance, respect, and loyalty to the living God as they move into adolescence.

SOMEONE TO LISTEN

One of the important functions of a good friend is that of listening attentively and caringly as the person struggles to conceptualize and communicate innermost thoughts. Older school-age children may find this intimacy with their closest peer friends, those with whom they share the secrets they would never share with anyone in the adult world. Younger children, kindergarten through third or fourth grade, will still depend on a parent who can listen without judgment. But all children can profit from having some other trusted adult who will listen. As we shall address again in later chapters, it is difficult for children to make conversation with adults, much less share intimate thoughts. They learn early that some of their words and ideas can threaten adults, so they learn to keep quiet or at least censor what they say. It is difficult, furthermore, for children to know how to describe their innermost thoughts and feelings.

When children find an adult whom they can trust with their innermost thoughts, yet feel accepted and liked anyway, they have found a real treasure. In this trusted relationship they are more likely to ask the deeper religious question, share the heaviest doubt, express the biggest fear, and confess the debilitating guilt or shame. You know from personal experience how much relief, freedom, and renewal can be experienced as a result of having some trusted person "hear you out." The final four chapters of this book give specific methods both for enabling children to communicate and for developing your capacity to listen.

SOMEONE TO ACCEPT THEIR FEELINGS

It is easy to forget that children, like adults, have feelings. Children are emotional selves who experience the full range of excitement, anger, grief, joy, anxiety, fear, affection, and guilt. If we are to relate to children as whole persons, and listen as thoroughly as we described above, we must take seriously their capacity for feeling.

Children's emotions can be threatening to adults. It is not easy for an adult to respond with concern and sensitivity to a child who is agitated, excited, angry, or even passionate. This reflects the adult's need to control his or her own emotive responses and is a projection of his or her own fear of emotions. In any case, children often hear admonitions such as, "Now, now, don't cry," or "You shouldn't be angry like that at your brother!" or "Don't be afraid, you're too old for that," or "Calm down, don't get so excited." Each of these statements discounts the child's emotional response and communicates that the emotive content of life is not good. Children often connect their feelings with their "bad self" and grow up trying to suppress feelings which, as they perceive them, are not acceptable to important adult figures.

One important goal of caring for children in crisis is that of providing an opportunity for them to express the emotive content of their trauma. We can provide a safe context for feelings to be described, felt, and discussed without fear of disapproval.

Because of this ambivalence about children's emotions, and of course their own, adults will often veil their own emotions from children. The pastor in appropriate ways can offer a different model by sharing feelings of grief, anger, affection, and joy. By allowing your emotional self to be available to children, you are blessing this good aspect of God's creation. Furthermore, children are drawn to genuine humanness, and the emotional self is part of being human. I have found that being a real person emotionally has contributed positively to my relationships with children. I might add that children will handle your emotions sensitively. You can trust them with your feelings.

SPIRITUAL GUIDANCE

Like adults, children raise theological questions and face challenges to their budding faith during crises. They may have more difficulty verbalizing these questions, and they may use a different vocabulary, but the importance of receiving guidance is very real. Why? School-age children are in a period of spiritual growth and development. They are disciples in the making. They are hearing and learning a number of ideas about God from parents, culture, church, school, and peers. They now have the intellectual capacity to string these pieces of information and single images into broader concepts about God.[26] As they progress past seven or eight years of age, they begin to think theologically, even if they do not know what "thinking theologically" means.

Children do not have a history of personal religious experience upon which to call. In the face of a crisis this leaves them vulnerable to the religious interpretations that they hear from others or that they make themselves. We have said earlier that children need to have their perceptions confirmed and their feelings named. This is particularly true as they develop concepts about their faith. It is important for children to have names for their religious perceptions: grace, blessing, mystery, salvation, sin, and forgiveness. These are only a few of the words that school-age children can assign to specific perceptions they have during a crisis.

A major responsibility of pastoral care during a crisis is making Christian theology understandable to the children. It is important to remember that this is not a different theology but is one that is communicated in such a manner that it takes into consideration the child's cognitive abilities and psychosocial understandings at each stage of development.[27]

The normal psychosocial needs and developmental tasks of the school-age child, which have been briefly described above, are challenged, exacerbated, and threatened by crises. Self-esteem is on the line and children need a solid, safe, trusted personal relationship in which to process their experiences. They need to explore their thoughts and feelings about the events or life situations that have produced the crisis.

It is particularly important for children to have an opportunity to explore the religious concepts and ideas that they ascribe or assign to each aspect of the crisis and then to conceptualize the spiritual meanings which they ultimately carry away from the entire experience. The significant adults in a child's life may not have the time, patience, sensitivity, awareness, or emotional reserves to provide such a relationship. You, the aware pastor, can be the one who is interested and takes the time to listen sensitively, to care for, and to enter into constructive conversation. This is one of the cups of cold water you offer the child in Christ's name. We turn now to the basic principles upon which to base such a ministry.

4

SOME BASIC PRINCIPLES
OF PASTORAL CARE
TO CHILDREN

Becoming more aware of how children have been overlooked, recognizing the significance of pastoral ministry with
children, and knowing what children need in crises may challenge you to reassess your ministry. Realizing the potential
influence you can have on school-age children may have gener-
ated excitement about committing time and energy to pastoral
care of them. If so, our next task is to examine the ways and
means of providing such care and allowing your pastoral personhood and your professional abilities to become a resource
for the children in your church.

The primary prerequisite for effective ministry with children
is that of loving them and being willing to get involved with
them in appropriate ways, as described below. Certainly you
want to be competent, so gaining a basic level of knowledge
and understanding will guide your plunge into relationships
with children. You can become significant to children by
choosing to be present with them, by learning how to communicate effectively with them about their concerns, and by being
free to enjoy their presence.

In Part II we will describe and illustrate specific ideas for
relating to children in crisis that will ease your anxiety and
allow you to take a leap of faith in your pastoral skills. First,
however, we will describe in this chapter some basic principles
for pastoral care with children.

GETTING STARTED

If children have not been a focus of your pastoral attention, it would be good to develop some ways of getting to know them and allowing them the opportunity to know who you are. It is much easier to be effective in caring for a child during a crisis if you have already established a relationship that is personal rather than distant. Developing a disciplined approach to the care of these young parishioners sets the stage for the significant interventions that are necessary in a crisis. Below are a few ideas for getting started.

Being with Children

The first order of business is to spend more time with children. Within the church this can be done by visiting in their Sunday school classes, showing up at vacation Bible school, and going to their camps and on their retreats. You can also take advantage of "bump into" situations. Your "marketplace ministry" provides those serendipitous contacts and conversations which occur on the street, at the softball game, in the store, at a church social, or in the front yard as you drive through a child's neighborhood. These three-minute interactions, many of which are humorous or lighthearted, are important in developing your relationships with children. They establish you as an adult friend in the mind of the child.

Children will also enjoy being around you while you are doing projects at the church. They like being helpful and demonstrating competence. Thus, to "employ" them to help with something at the church, in your home, or in some service to others will accomplish several goals. Children can even accompany you on your pastoral visits to other children, particularly if they have been through a similar crisis.

Talking with Children

Be intentional about relating to children in a personal manner so that they realize you are genuinely interested. Try an easy experiment. Decide that each Sunday for a month you will engage two children in conversation (beyond saying hello). Take time in the corridor, vestibule, or parking lot to focus full attention on that child. "Hello, Elizabeth, how are things going at school?" "What is happening at your house this week?" "What special projects are you working on?" "Tell me what Paul, your new little brother, is doing these days." "I hear your grandfather is living with you now. How are things different for you?"

Questions like these will lead to a few minutes of private conversation which solidifies your relationship. Feel free to call a child apart from the rest of the family in order to show that you recognize the child as a unique individual. If you have decided that spending time and energy with children is a valuable way of *giving* yourself to ministry and fulfilling the shepherding task, you will not worry about the adults you are *not* seeing.

Be sure to speak like a normal adult. You don't have to come on like Ronald McDonald or the television children's hostesses with their hyped-up excitement and exaggerated voices. You do not have to be different in order to hold a child's attention. You are representing the real world and they will respond.

Leading Worship and Teaching

If you have never led a separate "children's church" or "children's worship," nor included a special "children's time" in a Sunday worship service, you are missing a treat. Taking the time to develop such a ministry will be meaningful to both the adults and the children of your parish. It is an excellent time to tell stories (see chapter 7). I am not the only pastor who has felt that the truths proclaimed in our "children's sermon" were remembered more clearly by the adults than the supposedly deeper messages that came later in the worship hour. Perhaps even more important than the content of such experiences is the clear establishment of your identity as a pastor to the children. When you focus your role as a leader of worship around a time for the children, it not only becomes symbolic of all your roles as the shepherd but conveys that you are *their* pastor, too.

Many pastors have an exciting opportunity to establish more meaningful relationships with children through their confirmation classes, although by this time the children are often into puberty and the opportunity to minister to them as children is almost gone. The pastor can establish special classes for school-age children and teach brief series in the Christian education program if he or she wants to begin knowing the children more personally.

Pastoral Notes and Telephone Calls

You can communicate your interest to children through written notes and telephone calls around special occasions. Some pastors write a note or make a telephone call on the child's birthday. It takes only a few minutes, but it contributes to the child's awareness of your involvement in his or her life.

Telephone calls at other celebrative times can also be meaningful. For example, you might call the day before a child is to welcome home a new baby brother or sister to say how excited you are that the child has a new responsibility as a big brother or sister and affirm his or her ability to do the job well.

Pastoral Visits

Although the art of pastoral visitation seems to be on the wane, it is still the most comprehensive manner of getting to know your parishioners. When you do visit a family, be sure that the children perceive that you include them in the family. Talk to them as well as to the adults. Let them introduce themselves to you. A brief pastoral visit to a child during a celebrative time models for the parents the importance of joy and affirmation.

WITH CHILDREN IN CRISIS

Now that you are being intentional in your pastoral care of children on a day-to-day basis you have a solid foundation for the care of children in crisis, the seeking, rescuing, healing roles of shepherding.

Who Is in Need?

It should go without saying that to provide pastoral care for children in crisis means knowing which children are in a crisis. This is not as easy as it may seem. First of all, children rarely seek out their pastor for help in a crisis. Second, the adults in your parish may have the same attitudes about children described in chapter 1 and therefore will not think to convey to you that a child is having a problem. This means that the initiative is in your hands—the ball is in your court. How can you keep up with "what is going on" with your young parishioners?

Parents. Make parents aware of your commitment to care for their children. Through pastoral letters, in parents meetings, and in church bulletins and newsletters, let it be known that you would like parents to inform you when their children are wrestling with any crises: (1) illness or hospitalization of a child or a family member, (2) death of any family member (including a pet) or family friend, (3) accident or trauma, (4) failure in school or personal relationships, or (5) major change in family life, such as unemployment, separation, or geographical move.

A good way to keep up with all parishioners is to take a "family inventory" whenever you talk with any member of the family. That is, ask how each member of the family is doing. You will often learn more from a concerned family member about others in the family than you would learn directly from the others. When talking with parents or with older siblings, ask specifically about the children. "How is Patty doing?" "What is happening in Roger's life?"

Christian Education Workers. Alert the individuals who teach in the church education program of your interest in ministry to children. Do not assume that they will automatically keep you informed. By and large, they will not perceive that pastors minister directly to children except in dire emergencies. They might also assume that you already know anything they would find out. These workers often overhear or receive information directly from the children about a lost pet, Grandpa's funeral, the neighbor's house catching on fire, or a mother's planned surgery. Through letters and teachers meetings ask them to keep you posted on any significant events they learn from the children. You need to be informed when the behavior of a child changes. When a child withdraws or begins acting up, it may mean there is a crisis in the family. You can involve the teacher in crisis ministry by inviting the teacher to visit with you, keeping teachers informed about what you learn, and discussing strategies for intervention.

The Children. Since you have begun to think of children as members of your parish and deserving of pastoral attention, you are talking with them in a more attentive and purposeful manner. When you talk with them now, you can learn from them about the critical events in their lives through the use of specific "How are you doing?" questions, which we illustrated earlier. As they learn to trust you and are assured of your concern for them, they will share their experiences with you.

Developmental Tasks. Keep track of the developmental tasks and the "marker" events in the lives of the children in your church. Who is going to first grade this year? When is the new sibling due? Who is having a birthday? When is she trying out for the school play? Such tasks are not only opportunities for the growth of the children but also possibilities for causing frustration, anxiety, and failure—in other words, a crisis.

Adult Crises. Remember, almost every time parents are in a crisis their children are also. If something is disrupting the parents' life, that same thing may be disrupting the child's life. If an adult is grieved, for example, his or her loss may be a loss for the child. If a parishioner's father dies, a child's grandfather has died. Think of other news you hear every week: Mr. Green is being transferred, Mrs. Smith was arrested for driving while intoxicated, the Lorenzos' home was burglarized, Joan's baby was stillborn, the Fasslers are separating. You will be offering pastoral care to these adults. Ask yourself if any children are involved. If so, recognize that they have had a potentially life-shaking experience and also need and deserve pastoral care.

Pastoral Initiative

After you have found out who is in need, the question of initiative surfaces. How can you reach out to a child in need? Actually, not much differently from the way you would with an adult.

Telephone Call. It is appropriate to call and talk specifically with the older child. "Hello, Janey, I heard yesterday that your grandmother died. It made me sad for you." Janey's response will depend on how well she knows you, how comfortable she feels with you, and, depending on her age and stage, her ability to conceptualize thoughts and feelings. If she does not respond with her own thoughts, you can pursue conversation with interchanges around questions such as, "What name did you call your grandmother?" "How did you hear the news?" and "When was the last time you saw her?" You do not have to talk for a long time to communicate your interest and set the stage for later encounters in which more profound conversation can occur.

Home Visits. We have already indicated how important it is when you are visiting in a home to include children in your visit. When a crisis has occurred, make pastoral conversation with the child one of your specific goals. If parents shoo the children out of the room, it may mean they need to talk with you privately about their response to the crisis. Or they may assume that you don't want to be bothered. While you say good-by to the children (in order to see what the adults need) let them know you want to see them before you leave. "Where will you be, Rick, so I can see you in a little while before I leave?" In this way you have communicated to Rick that you are interested in him as an important person in his own right.

If children stay with the family during your visit, find a way not only to involve them in the conversation but to have a few private moments. "Leah, will you walk me to the car? I have something I want to tell you." This brief time also serves the purpose of symbolizing your interest in Leah apart from the family. It also gives you a chance to enhance the relationship with a statement such as, "I remember when my grandmother died, I was only one year older than you are. It was a sad time. I never saw my father cry until she died. I remember being a little bit afraid of going to the funeral home. What is it like for you?"

Your Office. Perhaps you have never invited a school-age child to your office for a conference, but it is quite proper to do so. Having the child come to the church makes it clear that you want to deal "officially" or "formally" with the crisis. Most children will feel honored to be taken seriously enough to be invited to your office. Some children may be apprehensive, but if the relationship is strong and you are able to make them comfortable with your friendly interest and concern, they will anticipate return visits.

Institutions. When working with children in crisis you will be seeing them at hospitals and funeral homes and at cemeteries. These are unfamiliar places to children and they may feel scared, lonely, anxious, or at least uncomfortable. Taking initiative at such a time reassures the children, symbolizes their inclusion, and reduces their sense of being a stranger.

Several days ago I was at a funeral home attending to a family whose five-year-old daughter/sister had died. My relationship with the two brothers, seven and eleven years of age, was new. How could I spend some private time with them? At one point I moved near the seven-year-old, leaned over and whispered in his ear, "Michael, I'm thirsty—have you found a water fountain in this place?" Of course, as any seven-year-old, he had completely explored the premises. "Yeah, come on and I'll show you!" he said. He not only took me to the water fountain but showed me the Coke machine and the coffeepot (not the one for guests but the one for employees!). I got us both a Coke and invited him to join me on a vacant couch. I asked specific questions about what was happening next and his part in the proceedings. He had the opportunity to tell me proudly that he would be one of the pallbearers at the cemetery and was promised he could be the last one to touch the casket before it was lowered into the ground. We became friends, which allowed me to offer meaningful pastoral care during the next months as he processed his grief.

Appointments

It is quite appropriate to make appointments with children for either personal visits or extended telephone calls. Structuring a time will let them know how seriously you take their concerns. It is courteous to their parents and lets the children know that their time is important to you. The child can then anticipate the visit or the telephone call. I usually let the child know the specific activity (see the chapters that follow) in which I want us to engage. I also find that being direct with children about the purpose of my visit helps. "I want to talk with you about your grandfather's death, Mike. May I see you at three o'clock tomorrow afternoon?"

Place

As a pastor you have cared for people in a variety of settings: living rooms, hospitals, funeral homes, your office, restaurants, sidewalks, and church parking lots. Where will you care for children? These same places plus two distinct additions: the child's room (or play place) in the home and the educational space at the church. Let me elaborate.

It is quite natural for most adults to feel comfortable talking with you in their living room or in your church study. Such places, however, are *not* natural for the child, certainly not for the five- to ten-year-old! With adults who are uncomfortable in formal settings, you often visit in *their* natural habitat (the garden, workplace, kitchen, backyard) or on neutral territory (a restaurant). In the same manner, relating to children is much easier when you get in their environment, where they feel at ease.

Home. When you are visiting a child at home, for example, find out where the child spends the most time. "Susan, when you are home, where do you spend most of your time?" She may lead you to the den, television room, garage, basement, backyard, or her room. Actually she will probably show you several places, which familiarizes you with her "turf." After the tour you can ask, "Where is the best place to talk?" Following her lead will put you in the place where she can be most comfortable.

If you have a certain methodology in mind that involves playing games or drawing (see chapters 5 and 6), you might need to ask her to choose a place with a table and chairs. You might also wish to include other family members, which means you might have to choose a neutral place. The kitchen table is often ideal, because it is neutral, informal, comfortable, and parents can be naturally present. When weather permits, going outside provides many children with more freedom to converse about important things.

Pay attention to parental concern about how much time you are spending with a child in an out-of-the-way place. Tell the parents what plans you and the child make so you will know whether it is all right with them. Set time limits so the parents know what to expect. Leave doors open. Children are rarely self-conscious about being overheard through open doors. Most of the time your pastoral conversation will be something in which other siblings and parents would participate anyway.

Church. When you invite children to the church, think about their age, comfort level with you, and how freely and easily they talk. Some older children will feel comfortable in your study and feel privileged to be there. Other children, particularly those under nine or ten, will feel out of place sitting in a large wing chair, or lost on a big, stuffed couch with their feet sticking straight out or dangling over the edge. Take them down to the educational space in the church. Here the child is in familiar territory. Chairs and tables are just the right size, even if a little uncomfortable for you. Here you have access to paper, crayons, chalkboard, puppets, play area, and games, all of which you may use to facilitate pastoral conversation, as we will describe in later chapters.

Remember, bringing children to your office should be done with parental knowledge and consent. If you have no secretary, arrange for the parent to stay nearby so that no questions can be raised about the propriety of the visit. A child might live close enough to come by on the way home from school or ride over on a bike later. Parents can leave one child while they take another child to a lesson.

How Much Time?

Adults are fairly easy to schedule: half-hour appointments for minor concerns, brief consultations, and "checkup" visits; full hours for formal counseling sessions and crisis intervention. It is not as easy with children. Yet, if you are intentional in both making an appointment with a child and structuring the visit for serious conversation (see the chapters that follow), then thirty minutes to an hour can be used to good advantage. How much time will depend on the child's age, attention span, level of interest in talking with you, outside distractions, and whether or not other family members get involved (the more family involved in the activities described later, the more time it takes). Stay as long as something creative is happening or until your schedule interrupts. To spend more than an hour would be unusual and probably unnecessary. Remember, even ten-minute visits can be meaningful to a child.

REFERRALS

The pastor who expends time and energy caring for children —keeping up with them, relating to them, listening to their secrets, watching their behavior—will encounter a few who need specific help in order to keep their growth and development on track. It is important to know where to turn for resource persons who can provide what children need to continue "becoming."

From the Family of God

When the need is for a substitute family member, the help may come from within the local congregation. Many children have lost a significant person in their lives because of death, divorce, or geographical separation. They may desperately need a substitute father, mother, brother, sister, or grandparent. They may find a natural replacement at school, in the neighborhood, or through the extended family, but if not, you may help them find one within the family of God.

Heidi is an eleven-year-old girl who, along with her two younger brothers, is being raised by her father. Her mother died from an undetected blood clot after a surgical procedure. This thirty-three-year-old father is doing well, but as Heidi moved into puberty, he and the pastor were aware that she needed a female model and confidante. She is learning more specifically now what it means to be a woman. She is grappling with new physical, social, and emotional realities. One of Heidi's Sunday school teachers was a forty-one-year-old woman whose older daughter was away at college and whose younger daughter was a junior in high school. The pastor talked with them about Heidi's need for a mother figure and an older sister to fill the female gap in her home. They were willing to take Heidi's life into their own and, with the father's wholehearted support, made an intentional effort to involve her in typically female-to-female situations. They took her shopping to buy her clothes, had her spend the night, helped her plan a party, and talked about sexuality and heterosexuality over the two-year period prior to her father's remarriage.

From the Professional Community

Other children will develop emotional problems that need the attention of a specialist in the mental health field who works with children. Ideally you will get to know the professionals in your community who work with children, just as you keep close ties with those to whom you refer adults for psychiatric consultation, psychological testing, psychotherapy, marriage and family therapy. Who are the psychologists, psychiatrists, pastoral counselors, social workers, marriage and family therapists in the local community or a nearby city who work with children? Find out from your network of mental health professional friends who these experts are and get to know them. One of the best ways to get acquainted is to call them for consultation or invite them to speak in your church. If your church has no consultation budget, swap a lunch for some supervisory conversation about the children in crisis you are caring for at the moment.

Specialized agencies, such as child guidance clinics and family and children's agencies, also take care of children and their families who have special needs. Some self-help groups are also a valuable resource. Our local chapter of Compassionate Friends (the international self-help group for bereaved parents) has a "sibling group" for children who have lost a brother or a sister by death.

Referrals, of course, should be considered within the context of pastoral conversations with the parents or responsible adults. They will usually share your concerns about the child. In fact, they may have introduced you to the particular problem in the first place. At other times, behavioral problems in the church or in school, or concerns the child reveals during pastoral conversation with you, may lead you to initiate contact with the parents. This may catch the parents off guard especially if they have been denying that a problem exists. You can help them know that early assessment and treatment can prevent later problems.

Follow-up

Please remember that pastoral care does not end when a referral is effectively accomplished. It is easy simply to ask the parent on Sunday how things are going, but pastoral care to the child is still necessary and appropriate. Telephone calls and visits with the child who is in therapy enables him to tell you what happens in his therapy sessions, what he is learning, what he likes and does not like about the therapist. You may choose to consult with the therapist (with the parents' permission) to find out the specific therapeutic goals that you can support. You may be able to provide information and insight that will help the therapist. By supporting the work of the therapist, you give your blessing to growth and self-discovery. The therapist is probably not making religious interpretations of the process, which is where you can make unique contributions.

MISCELLANEOUS HINTS

Relating to children is not as difficult as you might suppose. Most of the principles that you follow when relating to adults are applicable to children. Here are a few ideas that may help with the differences.

Respecting Psychological Space

Do not get too physically close too quickly when first meeting children. Like adults, they have social and psychological "territory" which needs protection. Because you are physically larger and represent the authority of the adult world, they may need more "psychic space" and time before feeling comfortable to let you get close. So, at the hospital stand in the doorway a moment and then at the foot of the bed until the relationship is under way or reestablished. At a child's home, sit on the other side of the room. If you wait, the child will symbolize her increasing comfort by finding excuses to move closer to you. She will bring something to show you or simply move to a closer chair.

Children will not appreciate touch until they invite you into their territory. Save your handshake or your touch on the arm until the end of your visit, or certainly until the rapport between you is clearly established. Then the touch can feel affirming and serve as a blessing rather than an invasion of personal space.

Physical Parity

Because younger children are physically small, they must always literally look up to adults. This places unnecessary physical and psychological distance between you and these younger folks. You can overcome this barrier by stooping or kneeling to their level or by inviting them to sit beside you. You will be amazed how quickly children respond to an adult who dares to get close to the ground. They recognize that such an act signifies a genuine desire to communicate with them.

If you doubt this, try a simple experiment. The next time you are in a funeral home where children are in attendance, kneel down near one child and begin a conversation. Within minutes other children will have noticed (instinctively it seems) and made their way to your side. Like a magnet you will draw children from all corners of the room. You can try the same thing in a church corridor or the fellowship hall.

Shared Activity

Focusing on something "outside" the child minimizes the child's anxiety at the beginning of a visit. Sharing an activity, such as playing a game of Ping-Pong, creating something unique to drink, getting introduced to a pet, or learning how a toy works, provides some opportunity for relaxed socializing. Ask children to show you their favorite toy or teach you their favorite game. Such activity puts little pressure on children and allows them to get comfortable. Actually, shared activity is an important and effective departure point for the pastoral care of children. The last four chapters of the book deal in depth with the use of play, storytelling, art, and writing as means and methods of pastoral care with children.

Speaking Directly to the Child

At times it becomes difficult to talk or relate to children because the parents jump in and speak for them. This is most likely to happen with a shy child or a sick child whom the parent wants to protect. Parents can become quite anxious if their child is not quick to speak to the pastor. "Speak up, Jimmy, the pastor asked you a question." "Say something, Lisa. Rev. Smith is here to visit with you." This will strain the relationship, of course, frustrating you and putting stress on the child. When this happens, protect the child with, "Jimmy might need to think that over while you and I are talking," or "Don't hurry, Lisa, we can talk later." Then turn and talk with the parents until they are more at ease. Explain that you now want to share a few things with the child. You can even suggest to adults in the room that you would like some private time with the child. If you are in a hospital, suggest that they take a fifteen-minute break at the snack bar and you will stay until they return. At their home you can suggest that you and the child find another place to talk.

If you have planned an activity such as those we will describe in the last chapters, you will be able to draw the family into the pastoral conversation. But if you want private time with the child, the parents are more likely to leave you alone if they know you have an activity planned with their child. As the child looks forward to visits with you, the parents' anxiety will also diminish.

THE PASTOR'S PERSONAL PREPARATION

Your pastoral care of children will be influenced and affected, like everything else in life, by your own experience as a child. Preparing for ministry to children can profitably include some evaluation of your own childhood days. What philosophy did your parents have about the place of children in the family? How did they choose to relate to you? Do you agree with their philosophy and manner of relating to children? Or will you need to be different in order to have a creative ministry with children?

If your parents' philosophy included, for example, the idea that children were to be protected from critical events in the family, they probably hid significant information which only became known to you in young adulthood. You may be tempted to follow this same philosophy without thinking it through. However, we know that children handle a crisis more effectively when they are given the data necessary to understand the situation. To minister effectively means you will have to become comfortable with allowing children to share the available information.

Another example could focus on whether or not your family of origin allowed the children to express emotion. If they did not, you may find it difficult even today to let others know what you feel. This means it will not be easy for you to offer pastoral care to children, since pastoral care ideally includes granting permission to express emotional responses to a crisis. To be effective with children will mean working to change your perceptions of what is appropriate for children to feel and express, so you can give this important freedom to children.

Caring for children effectively includes the willingness to identify with the child's hurt, vulnerability, fear, anger, and sense of loss. To empathize with the child, to "hang in there" in the face of his or her pain, can only be managed if you have been willing to claim your own personal pain. You must be willing to explore personal experiences with grief, loss, guilt, shame, fear, and danger, particularly if experienced as a child. If wounds from the past are left unhealed, it will be difficult for you to allow a child to deal openly with a crisis in your presence. The child's emotional pain will be too threatening to that which lies unresolved in one of your interior closets.

On the other hand, if you have been willing to examine your own childhood traumas, reliving them if necessary, bringing closure and resolution where possible, integrating that experience into your present sense of self-identity, then you will be able to facilitate a child's confrontation with the hurt and pain of crisis without becoming unduly anxious or overwhelmed by your own memories.

The principles of pastoral care described in this chapter are based on pastoral functions that you already practice. We have set the context for caring for children in crisis by redirecting familiar aspects of ministry toward children. These ideas can be quickly integrated into your ministry. Reaching deeper levels of pastoral care with children in crisis, however, calls for different methods of relating than we use with adults. Part II will explore some unique methods for conducting pastoral conversation with children.

PART II

METHODS OF PASTORAL CARE
OF CHILDREN IN CRISIS

5

THE USE OF PLAY IN PASTORAL CONVERSATION

The natural habitat of the child is the playroom. Anytime boys and girls are at play, they are doing that which is most natural to them. Play is to children what talk and work are to adults. It is their way of expressing themselves. In play activity they practice the process of being a human being and act out adult living. They experiment with and "try on" adulthood as they imagine it and experience it in their own environment. So we watch them dress up like adults and take on adult roles as they play house, doctor, and space shuttle.

Because play is the child's world, we must go into that world to gain most complete access to the child's thoughts and feelings. Erik Erikson says that play is "the royal road to the understanding" of children's perceptions of the world and their attempts to make sense of the world they perceive.[28]

CHILDREN AND PLAY

Persons who work with disturbed children have long used play as a major vehicle for therapy.[29] Play therapy is the structured use of play activity that allows children to project their inner perceptions onto objects in the playroom and express their suppressed emotions in what they perceive to be (and actually is) a safe context.[30] This process works well because children do not recognize that while playing they are revealing

85

so much about themselves. This allows them to reach a level of spontaneity in play which is difficult to attain in conversation with adults.

Talking directly with adults, even under normal circumstances, is not an easy task for most children. When they are under stress, or troubled and upset, it is even more problematic. They fumble for adequate and appropriate words to express themselves, question their own ability to make sense, and censor those thoughts and ideas which they think will upset the adult. As a result, they worry about being embarrassed by what they might say and often just stay quiet.[31] Every pastor has had the experience of initiating a conversation with a child who would not speak back. A painful experience for both pastor and child! This week I made an initial pastoral call to meet six-year-old Candice, who was in the hospital with a serious intestinal blockage. The nurse told me that Candice was usually verbal and felt well enough that day for conversation. However, when I tried to begin a dialogue she looked down at her bed or at the far wall. For several minutes I tried every "trick" I knew, all in vain. She was uncomfortable, caught off guard in some manner. Finally, I bid a weak, and frustrated, good-by, indicated that I would return later, and retreated in defeat.

In play activity, these inhibitions are reduced considerably. When children get into games and make-believe, the focus of attention moves away from direct interaction with the adult and they relax. When children do not feel "on the spot," as they often do when we talk directly with them, they can respond normally. In the process of play, they let us know more completely who they are and what they are up against.

As you can imagine, playing with children is a helpful way of establishing rapport. Since a first step, and a crucial one, in the pastoral care of children is establishing a warm, comfortable, "I understand your world" relationship, play can be a most helpful vehicle. When I went back the second time to see Candice, I took my trusty puppet and the visit went much better, as I will describe later. In your Children's Kit, carry a box of dominoes, a pack of UNO cards, or any other game that you enjoy playing with children. You will find that most children respond when you ask, "Would you like to play UNO?" If they haven't played before, it is easy to teach and fun to play. More important, it is easy to socialize and get to know each other while playing a few hands. These games do not create the same openings for significant pastoral conversation as those described below, but they serve well in establishing the relationship.

What children reveal through play enables the child therapist to make more accurate diagnostic evaluations. Pastors must also be interested in making assessments. We must know what children are thinking and feeling if we are to understand their perceptions and interpretations of a current crisis. Play therapists spend most of their time watching and observing, which is most appropriate for the preschool child. The pastor, however, will find it most helpful *to participate with* the children in their play (an incarnational dimension). This personal engagement suits our goals and objectives better than the detached observation method, for we want to focus our pastoral care on a particular life event. We are also talking about pastoral care to school-age children who are a little older on the average than those with whom the play therapist works.

Play is helpful not only in establishing rapport and making pastoral assessments but also in opening up pastoral conversation within which other pastoral tasks, such as expression of emotion, reality testing, and teaching, may be accomplished. The play therapist uses play for these purposes and so may the pastor, as we will illustrate in the sections that follow.

PUPPETS

Children love puppets. They humanize them and invest them with character and personhood. Younger children will relate to puppets as if they were alive, and older children are glad to join in making believe that they are real. Interacting with puppets is play; therefore children do not feel as threatened talking *to* a puppet or *through* a puppet as they feel when talking directly to an adult. Children reveal more about themselves through a puppet, because they do not realize it is the same as talking directly to the adult.

Carry several puppets in your Children's Kit. Neuter ones are most practical, although using male and female puppets can expand the range of interaction. Children will give gender to the puppets if they need to. However, much can be accomplished through the neuter puppets, without the unconscious baggage the child might associate with either gender.

One Puppet

At the appropriate point, introduce the younger child to your puppet "friend" by name (a neuter name like Sunshine or Rainbow is best). Then let your "friend" talk directly to the child. If you make believe that the puppet is doing the talking, by looking directly at it and making its mouth move as close as possible to your syllables, the child will talk to the puppet. You do not have to pretend ventriloquism by hiding lip movement, although a change in voice tone can be helpful.

The puppet, of course, will conduct an interview that you have planned in the light of the child's situation. For example, my second visit with six-year-old Candice included some conversation between my puppet and me which I hoped would keep Candice off "the spot" until she felt free to get involved.

PASTOR: Hello, Candice, I want you to meet my friend Fuzzy, who is visiting with me today. Fuzzy, this is Candice. I met her yesterday, but we aren't friends. Yet. *(Candice looks at the puppet, but says nothing.)*

PUPPET: Hello, Candice, nice to meet you. *(To pastor)* Rev. Lester, why did you say Candice was in the hospital?

PASTOR: *(To puppet)* Her stomach was hurting, Fuzzy.

PUPPET: You mean like a stomachache?

PASTOR: I think so, but it is not hurting as much now.

PUPPET: *(Puppet is inspecting IV tube in Candice's arm and then says with some concern in voice)* Rev. Lester?

PASTOR: Yes, Fuzzy?

PUPPET: What is that string going into Candice's arm?

PASTOR: That is an IV, a little tube that is carrying food and medicine into her body.

PUPPET: Into her arm? Oh my? *(With concern)* Does it hurt, Rev. Lester?

PASTOR: I don't know, Fuzzy, you will have to ask Candice.

PUPPET: *(To Candice)* Candice, does that tube hurt your arm?

CANDICE: *(To puppet)* Not too bad.

PUPPET: *(To Candice)* How did they get it in there?

Candice became involved in conversation with Fuzzy at this point and talked another ten minutes. Let me list some of the other questions that Fuzzy asked and that Candice addressed in a way she might not have if I had asked directly: "What happens to you in here every day?" "When does it get scary in here?" "What is it like at night?" At the end of the conversation, Fuzzy asked if they could be friends now and if it would be okay to come back with Rev. Lester again. Candice smilingly said yes and invited Fuzzy to come back the next day.

Another visit Fuzzy made might illustrate how a conversation between pastor and puppet can be used to teach, or remind, a child of something about our faith. Thomas was a seven-year-old boy hospitalized with leukemia. He had been frightened by the experience, was having difficulty sleeping, and did not want his mother to be absent. The family was active in a Methodist church and Thomas went to Sunday school regularly. The following took place just after Thomas had admitted to Fuzzy that he got scared the previous evening.

PUPPET: If I were here at night, I would probably be scared too.

PASTOR: Fuzzy, do you remember what you learned in Sunday school?

PUPPET: About being scared?
PASTOR: About God watching out for children. And when
           a child is scared, like Thomas, God will be
           around to help us feel brave.
PUPPET: In the hospital?
PASTOR: Yes.
PUPPET: I thought God was at church.
PASTOR: Yes, but God can go anywhere.
PUPPET: *(Slowly looking around the room)* I don't see God.
PASTOR: No, God is invisible, like the wind, but believe
           me, God is here.

My purpose, of course, is to remind Thomas that we believe
God is present. Whether you would convey this same message
or some other, it illustrates what you can use a puppet to
accomplish. If I had been Thomas' regular pastor and he had
seen me lead worship, the impact of such a message would
have been even stronger. It should also be pointed out that a
child younger than school age would not have the intellectual
ability to understand correctly such a conversation about God.

Two Puppets

Children, particularly those seven to ten years of age, will
take on the identity of a puppet. While making up the words
they let the puppet say, they don't realize completely that they
are really sharing out of their own thoughts and feelings. They
project their own struggles into both the character and the life
situation which they grant the puppet.

You need to carry more than one puppet in your Children's
Kit to do this. Introduce your puppet. Then give the other
puppet to the child, with clear instruction to give it a name so
that your "friend" can talk with the child's "friend." I usually
assign a situation and set the scene. Let me describe a visit in
the home of eight-year-old Vernon, who had recently been to
his grandfather's funeral. While at the funeral home he had
become upset and bolted from the premises. I introduced Vernon to my puppet, telling him that Fuzzy had never been to a
funeral and wanted to learn what it was like. Then I gave him

the other puppet and told him that his puppet *had* been to a funeral and I needed to help Fuzzy know what going to a funeral was like.

PASTOR: What is your puppet's name?
VERNON: *(After a pause)* Stinky?
PASTOR: Fuzzy, meet Stinky. Stinky has been to a funeral
          and is ready to tell you about it.
FUZZY: Hello, Stinky. You mean you went to a real
          funeral?
STINKY: Yes, my grandfather died.
FUZZY: What did they do?

Through Stinky, Vernon went ahead to describe the funeral. Fuzzy asked questions like, "Did people cry or anything?" and "Did you touch the body?" which elicited from Stinky some important data. Finally Fuzzy asked, "Did you get scared?" Stinky's reply was, "Yeah, I started thinking that my grandpa couldn't breathe in that coffin and I cried." Nobody in the family had known what had bothered Vernon, but he was able to describe it through Stinky.

THE UNGAME

A most delightful and productive resource for relating to children is the Ungame.[32] This is a normal-looking board game with playing pieces that the players move around on the board a certain number of spaces each turn, depending on the number thrown with dice. The game has a "start" but has no "finish," though the children rarely notice. The goal of this noncompetitive game is to facilitate communication among the group that is playing. In my experience, children take to it quickly and enjoy it thoroughly. It is an excellent means for involving a whole family in meaningful conversation about a crisis.

The game accomplishes its goal by providing three types of "space" upon which any player can land. One type is called "hang-up," which has written on it statements such as, "If you worried this week, relax on 'worry wharf'" and "If you felt lonely this week, take a vacation at 'cheerful chalet.' " Of course "worry wharf" and "cheerful chalet" are places on the board to which you move your playing piece. If the player moves his piece in response to a "hang-up," he tells the group his reasons—why he worried or when he felt lonely.

A second type of space is labeled "tell it like it is" and is related to the three stacks of cards that come with the game. One stack is called "lighthearted" and poses questions like these: "What would you do if you found $1,000 in a vacant lot?" "If you could become invisible, where would you like to go?" "What makes you feel frustrated?" A second stack is entitled "deep understanding" and asks more thought-provoking questions: "What do you think makes a marriage happy?" "Share a time when your feelings were hurt." "What is something that makes you angry?" The third stack is "Christian belief" and asks the player to respond to something about the Christian faith: "If you were asked to preach a sermon, what would the title be?" "What are three things that you believe about God?" "If you met Jesus face-to-face, what question would you like to ask him?" The player who lands on a space marked "tell it like it is" must choose a card from one of these stacks and answer the question. You can imagine how interesting children's answers to these questions might be! Each stack has blank cards upon which you can write your own questions. The manufacturer has other stacks of cards available. Of course, you could make your own stack of cards specifically for a group of children who were struggling with the crisis of parents divorcing or with any other specific crisis in which you wanted to use this game.

The third and last type of space on the board is called "do your own thing." Landing here gives the player permission either to make a comment or, as more frequently happens, to ask any other player a question. It is at this point that you can direct the game in ways that lead into pastoral conversation you think will be most productive for the child (or children if siblings are involved).

Recently I took the Ungame on a visit with a family whose youngest member, five-year-old Crissy, had died. I told the seven-, eleven-, and twelve-year-old brothers that I was bringing a game, so they could anticipate my visit. Our relationship was good and they played eagerly, sharing quite openly their responses to the questions on the cards. When my marker landed on "tell it like it is," I asked the youngest boy, "What do you remember most about the funeral?" His answer described the balloons that had been released at the cemetery symbolizing his sister's ascent. This led to a ten-minute discussion about where the sister was now. I learned about their childlike theology and could affirm the meaning behind some of their most important beliefs. Other questions that I asked during the game (only when landing on the "tell it like it is" space) included, "What do you miss most about Crissy?" (to the eleven-year-old) and "How are things different now?" (to the twelve-year-old). Discussion on each subject ran many minutes, and the fact that the game was delayed went unnoticed by three boys who needed to talk seriously about their dead sister. In this particular instance the father was present at the kitchen table and, although not playing the game, did participate creatively in this conversation.

The rule that allows a player who lands on "tell it like it is" to make a comment provides an opportunity for offering pastoral care through statements that instruct, affirm, or proclaim— all of which are goals for pastoral care with children. For example, with the brothers above I said on one occasion (after landing on a "tell it like it is" space), "I want to make a comment. I want to thank God that during her five years of life on earth, Crissy had three brothers who took care of her as well as the three of you did." I hoped this would be a blessing to them and affirm the realities that their parents had described.

There is one other interesting and instructive comment about the above situation. When we first sat down to play, the twelve-year-old was not sure it was a game in which he wanted to get involved. As you would imagine, he needed to protect himself from getting involved with something childish. My response to his ambivalent resistance was to say, "I think you will like it, Max, but I'm not sure. Why not play with us for five minutes by my watch. Then, if it isn't a game you enjoy, I'll understand and you can go do something else." When he got involved, of course, he played the entire forty-five minutes and was the one who asked me to bring the game back on another visit.

In short, this game is simple to play, yet can serve as a basis for profound pastoral conversation that seems natural to a child because it is taking place within a play situation. The children therefore rarely feel as inhibited as they would if the same subjects came up in a sit-across-from-each-other-in-chairs-and-talk type of conversation. One added benefit is that you will be more relaxed because you are having a leisurely pastoral conversation in which there are plenty of opportunities for you to digest what has been said and plan your next interaction.

THE BAG OF WORDS GAME

This game is described by Richard Gardner, the widely known child psychiatrist, in his excellent book, *Psychotherapy with Children of Divorce.* [33] The object of the game is to pull a word card out of a bag and either comment or tell a story about the word in order to win a chip. The game sparks the child's natural curiosity and excitement in the face of the unknown, like any grab bag game.

To create your own version, you will need the following:

1. A medium-size bag (a plain brown one from the kitchen will do) on which you have painted or drawn the title BAG OF WORDS GAME.

2. A pair of dice (one pair will be sufficient).

3. A small box of chips (poker chips or tiddlywinks chips work fine).

4. A small box or bag with a few inexpensive dime store prizes (sugarless gum, pencil, plastic jewelry, etc.). This bag or box needs to be clearly marked PRIZES.

5. Forty or fifty small cards (2″ x 3″ work well) and a felt-pen with which to write.

On each card you will print a word such as those listed below. These are words that will allow children to reveal through their comments and stories what they are experiencing. You will be using these same words to convey what you wish the child to hear through *your* comments and stories. You will develop your own list, but here are some examples:

dirty	adult	baptism
funeral	brave	dad
prayer	alone	operation
accident	punish	boy
divorce	mad	disease
friend	worry	die
crybaby	hospital	sorry
body	cuss word	grandfather
scared	hell	girl
afraid	love	teacher
mom	blame	ambulance
baby	stupid	bad
lucky	tease	cruel
heaven	sad	Jesus
happy	wish	church
fail	behave	anger
sick	God	grandmother

The rules of the game are simple. You and the child (and other family members if they are involved) take turns throwing dice. If a certain pattern (such as odd numbers, or even numbers, or if the dice total five or more, etc.) turns up, the player gets to reach in the paper bag and pull out a card. If the player will make any comment about the word (describe, define, or discuss it), he will receive one chip.

If, however, the player is willing to make up and tell a story about the word, he will receive two chips. Certain cards can be colored or marked in some way to indicate they are worth double chips. Or, a certain pattern on the dice can mean you lose a turn, or have to tell a story, or have to stand while commenting, or get a bonus turn, or anything else that will enliven the game and hold the child's interest. At the end of the game, which can be set with a time limit, the player with the most chips is allowed to choose a prize from the prize bag.

You can learn many things from children as they comment on or tell stories about these words. As with puppets and the Ungame, you may pursue secondary questions after a child finishes commenting or telling a story in order to help you clarify their thoughts and feelings. Asking for examples and illustrations enables the children to be more specific in identifying with the word or projecting personal experience into their responses. As you draw words, you can make comments or tell stories that affirm, inform, or present realities to correct any distortions that you have heard from the child, or accomplish any of the other goals of pastoral care with children described in chapter 3.

6

PASTORAL CARE THROUGH ART

The Creator has given us the gift of expression, the desire to symbolize what we think and feel through the creative activity we call art. The primitive art of our ancestors (drawings on cave walls and simple sculptures) probably developed before language and certainly before the written word. Visual art has always been a major vehicle for symbolizing the deepest human experiences. Art expresses the longings of our hearts, communicates our emotional needs, confesses our hopes and fears, and reveals our religious ideas. Art serves children in this same manner.

CHILDREN AND ART

Children are natural-born "artists," as any parent can confirm. Young children are enthralled by the marks that pencils and crayons (or their mother's lipstick) can make on walls, tables, and floors—sometimes even on paper we provide. "Creative" work with paint, crayons, or chalk can capture a preschool child's attention for a comparatively long time.

By the time children enter kindergarten they are more disciplined and sophisticated about using various modes of "art work"—paint, clay, chalk, felt-tip markers, cutting and pasting. Their motivation and enjoyment are still high. Art work is an excellent medium for self-expression and for learning, so it is used often at school and in Christian education programs.

Art is a unique form of self-expression because it does not depend on words and verbal skills. Most children feel limited by words anyway (aren't we all, as anyone who preaches regularly knows?). Children still have a limited vocabulary. The cognitive skills necessary for accurate and comprehensive verbal skills at the abstract level are not fully developed until later. Children are also sensitive to those thoughts and feelings which upset their parents (and, they assume, other adults), which means they limit what they express verbally. This self-censorship is often stronger in a crisis situation when the child realizes that the adults are already agitated.

The beauty of art work is that children express themselves more freely (if given permission), because they do not realize that their thoughts and feelings can be understood. They can communicate through art because it is so indirect. Children do not realize they are revealing important things about themselves to observers through what they draw or paint.

Brian, a nine-year-old whose family is not talking with him about the fact that his thirteen-year-old sister is dying with cancer, is a good example. The family believe that Brian is oblivious to the sister's situation and want to keep it that way. So Brian never uses words like "death," "dying," or "cancer" in his conversations with the family or the pastor. However, when I asked him to draw some pictures about "how things were going to be next year" (see "Draw the Future," in the section "Methods"), Brian drew one picture of a cemetery for children and another of his family on a vacation in which his sister did not appear. In conversation with me, Brian finally said, "Don't tell Mom and Dad, but I think my sister is going to die." Over the weeks to come, I was able to convince the parents that Brian needed to be brought into the family secret, and a ministry of reconciliation occurred.

Recognition of what art means to children and what art can reveal about them has prompted the rise of a new discipline called art therapy, which is also referred to as expressive therapy or creative therapy.[34] In the last forty years, art therapy has become an important technique in the care of disturbed children.[35] It is often used as an adjunct to other therapies (particularly those dependent on verbalization, such as traditional psychotherapy) and, in some instances, as the primary mode of therapy. Art therapists are adept at using a child's art work both as a diagnostic tool (helping assess the child's emotional and psychological situation) and as a therapeutic medium (helping children "work through" emotional conflicts by expressing themselves through art activity). Much has been written on the psychological interpretation of children's art, not only from form and content but from choice of color as well. It is not our purpose to become art therapists, but we can learn to use some of their methods to facilitate our pastoral care of children.

ART AND PASTORAL CARE

Since we know that art is meaningful to children and also know how they use art, we can describe some of the uses of art activity in our pastoral care of children.

Purposes

The more we know about an individual, about his or her unique internal world, the more effective we can make our pastoral care. Art activity allows children to reveal more of what they think than they might reveal with verbal skills. Children will also express more feelings and emotions through art than they might feel comfortable expressing verbally. We will learn more, therefore, about (1) how the child is *observing* and *perceiving* the external world, particularly the events that have sparked the crisis, (2) how the child is *interpreting* these events, and (3) how the child is *responding* internally to these events.

Art can serve the pastor as a vehicle for communicating reality to children which will help them cope with crises and strengthen personhood in the face of stress. The pastor can use communication around art work (1) to change the child's perspective or interpretation of events, (2) to confirm or affirm something about the child which serves as a blessing, or (3) to convey something about the Christian faith that will accomplish either of the above and set a solid foundation for the development of spiritual insight.

When to Use Art

When would you choose to use art? Like some types of play activity, art activity is a good icebreaker, something to create a relaxed and safe atmosphere while you are getting acquainted and the child is learning to trust your presence, evaluate your intentions, and feel comfortable interacting with you. An illustration of structuring an initial conversation through art is given under "Free Drawing," in the section "Methods."

A second use of art is in structuring an interview or a visit with a child. This afternoon I will be visiting sisters, eight and eleven years of age, who are suffering through a difficult bereavement over their older sister's death. When leaving them last week, I told them that when I came back today we would be drawing some pictures. I even asked them to have their crayons and paper ready. When asked what we would draw, I told them I would give specific instructions when I returned. This announcement created a sense of anticipation about my visit today and gives me a clear structure in which to have pastoral conversation with these girls.

Art activity can be very helpful when conversation "trips" over a certain topic—that is, you find some resistance in the child for pursuing a particular line of thought. Some of the art work methods described on the following pages can serve as a nonverbal path into the particular area where the child is hesitant to go verbally. In these instances, art serves to expand certain interactions and provides a way for the child to deal with something too important to skip over.

At other times, especially with older children, you can assign art work as "homework." Assigning a particular task (any of those mentioned in the next section, "Methods") gives children an opportunity before your next visit to think about their crisis and explore some aspect of it through art. It saves you time, yet is available at the next visit for a conversation starter. Some children who like art will take these assignments very seriously and communicate things to you that might not be revealed if you were depending only on the verbal conversation as a medium of pastoral care.

This "homework" use of art can also serve as an evaluative

tool. You might ask, "Jason, I want you to draw me a picture in the next several days that shows the most important thing we have talked about today." When you see Jason's picture and hear his explanations you will know what impact your visit had. Another way of checking Jason's progress is by giving him the same assignment you gave him a month ago and see whether there are any differences that reveal how his ideas or feelings are changing.

Occasionally an older child will protest, saying, "I can't draw very well" or "I don't like art work." This resistance may represent a concern that you, the pastor, would evaluate the child by his skill as an artist. Remember, school-age children are working to master their environment and like to be seen as competent and skillful. If this protest comes from an older male, it may represent his perception that art work is for "sissies." Usually you can overcome a child's reluctance by the reassurance that being good does not matter, because drawing is a way of talking. "Besides," you say, "I'm going to be drawing too, so we will agree not to laugh at each other's work but only to understand it." If the child is still reluctant, then switch to another mode of interaction, such as play or writing.

The Pastor's Participation

This method will be more effective if you participate in the art activity. You can imagine how uncomfortable children will be if you sit there watching them draw a picture. When structuring an art activity for them, also structure it for yourself. Tell them what you are going to do so they are aware of the mutuality of the assignment (examples are given in the section "Methods"). When you enter into the art activity, it gives them permission to get involved. They will usually take it as seriously as you do.

You can take as long as needed to finish the drawings or other art activity. It will depend on the child's skill level and range of interest in art work. I adjust my speed and amount of detail to the child's so that we finish about the same time and draw with roughly the same skill level. If the child draws stick people, so do I, but if the child fills out bodies and goes into detail, I do the same. (Of course, many children draw better than I, so in that case I just do the best I can and try not to get threatened. Luckily, children usually ignore my lack of talent or treat it with gentle humor.) Remember, you do not have to be a good artist—you only have to be willing to do what you can.

Furthermore, you will have to be willing to reveal your own thoughts and feelings (to the extent appropriate for a child) if you want the child to do the same. The level of your openness will set the stage for the child, and the family, to approach the same level.

Drawing in silence is fine; in fact, you might even suggest it when you have given a specific assignment. However, it is probably best to follow the child's lead. If the child is quiet and concentrating on the assignment, let it be; if he or she talks, respond. If the child's remarks are only passing the time of day, respond briefly so the focus remains on the art activity. But if the conversation is relevant to the crisis or the assignment, respond with all your active listening skills.

MATERIALS

The ideas suggested on the pages that follow do not require extensive equipment. In your Children's Kit simply stash a large package of felt-tip markers, a big box of crayons, and a package of plain paper (8½" x 11"). You can keep the same supplies in a desk in your office to use when children meet you at the church. Leave your kit in the trunk of your car so that it is always available for home and hospital visits. Most children, of course, have art supplies in their home and will be delighted to let you use them.

If art is something in which you are personally interested and with which you are comfortable, you can expand to including painting, sculpturing (with modeling clay, play dough, or pipe cleaners), making collages, and other modes of art.

METHODS

We turn now to specific methods for using art activity as a means of interacting with children. These ideas are geared particularly to the task of pastoral care with children and illustrate their use in achieving specific goals of pastoral conversation in crises.

Free Drawing

Art therapists are most frequently open-ended in their work with children, granting complete freedom for children to create whatever they want. This freedom allows children to reveal, in a more "free associational" manner, what is going on inside them.[36] There are times when the pastor will also want to be this unstructured. The simple approach is to ask the child to draw (or paint) a picture of anything he or she wants to draw. Choice of theme (subject matter), technique, and level of involvement (amount of detail and amount of time to use) are left up to the child.

This approach is particularly helpful in the beginning of your pastoral intervention if you do not know the child well. After introductory conversation, you can say, "One of the things I like to do is to draw. Let's find a table and draw some pictures while we talk. I have some felt-tip markers with me. Do you have any crayons or markers we could use?" When the child asks what to draw, it is simple to say, "Let's draw anything you want to draw." While drawing, you can get acquainted by talking about school, hobbies, friends, siblings, vacations, teachers, and television shows. Using this "free drawing" early gives you a chance to see how the child takes to art and whether or not it will be worthwhile to continue using art as a medium of interaction. It will also reveal how easily and how extensively the child deals with significant agendas through art.

Occasionally, for both diagnostic and therapeutic reasons, art therapists will become more structured and give specific direction to the child's artistic activity. Because the pastor's clear goal is to intervene in a particular crisis, and because he or she is usually dealing with normal children around a specific event of which both are aware, the pastor will usually find it more helpful to use structured techniques. For example, even in an initial contact such as described above, the pastor might give direction. When the child asks, "What should I draw?" the pastor could say, according to the crisis:

I understand you're going to move to Indianapolis. Why not draw a picture of what your neighborhood will be like when you move? (To an eight-year-old boy)

Draw me a picture about what is happening to you today. (To a nine-year-old in the hospital room)

Your mom's been in the hospital for two weeks now. Why not draw a picture about what home is like when she is gone? (To a ten-year-old girl whose mother was injured in a car wreck)

Can you make a picture of the fire that was in your home a few days ago? (To a seven-year-old boy)

Other structured techniques are the following:

Draw a Feeling

We established earlier (see chapter 3) that children, like all human beings, have feelings. Their responses to crises have the same intense emotional components as do the adults involved. The only difference is that children generally have more difficulty identifying and labeling their emotions. Their lack of experience may leave them confused about what to "name" their feelings. Furthermore, they may be reluctant to share what they do feel with adults. Therefore, an important goal of pastoral care is to enable children to identify, label, and express their emotions.

The "draw a feeling" art activity can be quite helpful. Ask the child to divide a piece of paper into four rectangles (by folding it twice or by drawing one vertical and one horizontal line through the center of the paper). Then ask the child to help you make a list of all the feelings you can think of—which may include scared, lonely, angry, embarrassed, happy, bad, sad, and so forth. After the list is complete, the following instructions are given:

"Now each of us will choose four of these feelings and draw a picture about each one in these squares. When we get through, we will look at each other's pictures and try to guess which feeling they show, so don't write the name of the feeling on the square."

After the pictures are finished, of course, take turns guessing which picture conveys which feeling. Then you can tell stories about each picture or describe why you chose to picture it that particular way.

Claudia Jewett illustrates a way of using art for these purposes with younger children (five to eight years of age). In her excellent book, *Helping Children Cope with Separation and Loss* (easy to read and full of valuable information for the pastor), she describes a way of helping children express their feelings. She calls it "The Five Faces Technique."[37]

She asks the child to help her get some paper ready and then asks the child to take five pieces and put one of the following words at the top of each sheet: sad, mad, glad (happy), scared, and lonely. Then after brief conversation with the child about how our faces tell people what is going on inside us, she asks the child to draw a face on each paper that goes with the word.

If the child is reluctant to draw, you can ease things by doing some drawing yourself, or, better yet, make some faces and ask the child to copy your expressions on the paper. This demands some freedom and spontaneity on your part. "If I looked like this, Jeremy, what would I be feeling inside?" "Right! Now try to draw this face I'm making." Or you can say to Jeremy, "That's how I look when I'm scared, how do you look?" Then when Jeremy demonstrates, you can draw a quick picture. Older children will even add bodies with postures that also reveal feelings.

After the faces are drawn, they can be used as a primer for storytelling. "Now, Jeremy, let's tell stories about these faces. Can you tell a story about some little boy or girl who has on a sad face?" After Jeremy tells a story, you can tell one that might be close enough to his life situation that he can identify with it and feel some of the emotion.

"Draw a feeling" can also be used to find out whether the child has any specific religious ideas concerning the situation. For example, you could say to the child, "I wonder what God's face looks like today. Would you draw a picture of what face God is wearing today?" If a child draws God with a mad face, you have an opportunity to ask the child to tell you why she thinks God is mad today. That could be followed by conversation around the question, "What could happen that would change God's face from mad to happy?" As pastor, you can offer interpretations of how God feels which can help children think of God in ways that direct their budding spiritual perceptions in healthy directions. "I drew a picture of God with a sad face because I think God is sad that your mother is so sick."

Picture the Problem

Shaping your ministry to meet the unique needs of each individual child requires an understanding of how each child perceives the crisis. Children can reveal much about how they view a crisis through their art. Asking them to "picture the problem" is a helpful way of focusing on how the *child* is actually perceiving the situation, which might be quite different from what the *adults* suppose. For example, here is a conversation with Sharon, a nine-year-old whose parents have separated and filed for divorce:

"Things have changed for you and your family, Sharon, but I'm not sure how. Things must be different for *you* since your mom and dad are divorcing. Will you draw me some pictures showing what it is like for you now? While you are drawing your pictures, I will draw some pictures showing what other children have told me about what it was like for them when their parents divorced."

After she finished her pictures, I asked her to tell me about what she had drawn. As Sharon explained the picture and answered some of my questions about parts of the picture, she gave me important clues about what she needs. Of course the very act of expressing her thoughts and feelings was helpful to her.

Meanwhile I drew pictures that visually represented what I have learned from other children about the impact of divorce on children: (1) being caught in the middle, (2) worrying if they caused their parents' problems, (3) being embarrassed about their family, (4) wondering why God let it happen, and so forth. After describing my pictures, I asked Sharon to tell me what parts she recognized as true for her. Her response added to my understanding of her inner struggles and also communicated to her that I knew some things about children caught in this crisis.

Picture Memories

Most crises, for children as well as for adults, involve *losing* some person or thing that was important. We know that grieving is a major aspect of crises involving separation and loss.[38] Furthermore, research shows that the process of remembering is an important part of creatively progressing through the grief process.

Having children make a picture of their memories enables them to reveal those aspects of the lost person or thing which they miss the most and long to have again. A child's pictures may reveal those things which the caring pastor needs to help the child replace or for which the child needs to find substitutes or surrogates.

I usually ask for more than one memory by dividing the sheet of paper into four quarters (either by folding or drawing lines) or giving several sheets of paper.

"Michael, I would like to have us draw some memories of your grandpa. What are some things you remember about him? I know you miss him, and I would like to have some pictures about what you miss most. Put a picture of a memory in each square (or on each piece of paper). I will draw some of my memories, too."

If other family members (particularly parents) are present, it can be quite creative to involve them in the same assignment.[39] When everyone is finished, you can ask each person to describe one of his or her pictures. If there is hesitancy, perhaps you can begin and establish a model for sharing both thoughts and feelings. As each person shares, the process of grieving is enhanced. Parents will learn how Michael is grieving, and Michael will learn about the content and emotion in his parents' grief.

Emotion may be strongly expressed as the stories are told and memories relived. If so, let it happen. The family will be brought together in their grief, which is reassuring to the child and grants the child permission to grieve within the family instead of in isolation. In fact, if any member of the family moves to cut off another's feelings, step in with a kind word that keeps it free: "It's okay for her to cry. Why don't you put your arm around her and let her use your shoulder?"

"Picture memories" can also provide an opportunity for communication around religious themes. You could, for example, share a memory you think God has of Grandpa (if Grandpa was a person toward whom Michael felt positive). You could say, depending on the age of the child and the realities about Grandpa:

"One of my picture memories tells one thing I think God misses about Grandpa. I remember how kind he was to the little children on Sunday mornings. He always smiled and played with them, which made them happy. I know God liked that and misses seeing Grandpa playing with the little kids. Do you?"

After Michael and the family respond to this, you can ask Michael (and other participating family members) to tell what he thinks God will miss about Grandpa. The stories they tell communicate that God is also feeling a loss. God's love for and empathy with the human situation is being indirectly proclaimed. This may calm fears that Michael may have about whether "God took Grandpa" and raise other possibilities about God's role in Grandpa's death. What you, as pastor, wish to convey will depend on what assurance about the faith Michael may need to hear, based on your other pastoral conversations with him.

If you choose to involve other members of the family, as in the example given, do not forget that the child is the focus of *this* visit. Keep the conversation focused on his thoughts and pictures as much as possible. You can have pastoral conversation with the adults about their particular grief at a later time.

Draw the Future

As indicated earlier, it is important to understand not only how the child *interprets* the current critical events in which he or she is enmeshed but also what he or she perceives to be the results or consequences of this crisis. How children view possible changes in the future probably has more impact on their response to the crisis than any other factor. Helping children conceptualize the future will most clearly reveal their fears and anxieties, since fear and anxiety are usually linked to the future. "Draw the Future" assignments can take numerous shapes.

Draw me a picture of what it will be like in your home after your father leaves. (To a nine-year-old boy whose parents were separating)

Show me in a picture what will happen between you and your grandfather the next time he comes for a visit. (To a ten-year-old girl who had been sexually abused by her grandfather)

Draw me a picture of what will happen during the surgery tomorrow. (To an eleven-year-old girl undergoing abdominal surgery)

Draw me a picture of what you will look like after the surgery. (To the same eleven-year-old girl)

This "Draw the Future" exercise is also effective in focusing attention on how the child can deal with the crisis—both the specific problems ("Picture the Problem") and the perceived consequences (above). When Sharon, whose parents are divorcing, identified with the picture I presented on "being caught in the middle," we talked about it. Then I asked, "How does that happen?" and she answered with some detail. After some discussion I said:

"It is tough to feel caught in the middle and I realize you want out of that spot. Let's draw pictures of some solutions. You draw one and I'll draw one and we'll compare notes."

The pictures focused discussion on ways that Sharon could cope with the crisis. The exercise enlisted her in taking initiative to imagine solutions. In drawing the pictures, she discovered an answer that made sense. Furthermore, through my pictures I had the opportunity to suggest solutions out of my experience which she had not imagined. After I discussed them with her, she considered them over a few weeks and tried several of them.

Occasionally a "Draw the Future" picture will convey death, destruction, or despair, which suggests that the child sees no workable future and has lost hope. If conversation confirms large amounts of hostility or depression, a professional referral would be the next step. Any sign that a child is not coping realistically, of course, should send you to your professional consultant or prompt a referral (see chapter 4).

Draw a Word

We have established that art is a major vehicle for helping children to reveal nonverbally their responses to traumatic, embarrassing, or frightening events which they could not or would not express verbally. In your pastoral conversations with a child, you may find that an aspect of a crisis has not surfaced or has not been addressed in any way. You might allow the child to explore this in a less threatening way through "Draw a Word." This particular exercise should be used only after your relationship with the child is well established and he or she illustrates this trust by sharing freely much of what he or she thinks and feels. It also works best if the two of you have already used art activities. You can introduce "Draw a Word" at an appropriate point in some manner such as this:

"Tommy, I've got a new idea for this afternoon. Words can be turned into interesting pictures, even though it's hard to do. Let's spend some of our time drawing words. We can take turns. One of us will think of a word and the other will take some time to draw a picture of the word. You go first."

Tommy will choose a word (which will probably be a thing, such as a frog or a horse) and you draw it. For your turn, choose a word that is not a thing, such as marriage, job, play, helping. After a few of those, you can choose a word that approaches the topic you wish the child to explore. "This time I want us to draw the word 'funeral' (or divorce, death, heaven, sick, bad)." The resulting picture will reveal some of

Tommy's thoughts and feelings which can be pursued both conversationally and by further art work.

THE USE OF ART IN PASTORAL CONVERSATION

Significant conversation may occur during an art activity, but it is more likely that the most meaningful sharing will take place after the drawings are finished. The previous section gives some specific illustrations, but here we will describe the principles for doing pastoral care through initiating pastoral conversation about the creative work of the child.

The Child's Interpretation

The most obvious response to a child's work is to ask the child for interpretation. An open-ended question that communicates real interest and curiosity will suffice: "Tell me what is happening in your picture." "Explain to me the different parts of the picture." "What were you thinking about while you were drawing?"

As the child talks, you will be thinking of questions that will elicit more of the child's inner thoughts and also clarify how the art work is relevant to understanding the child's response to the crisis. "Why is the dog barking?" "Why does the mother look so sad?" "What is the boy upset about?" "What made the little girl sick?" are examples of questions that extend the conversation and enable the child to interject more feelings and thought into the picture.

Storytelling

Another method that enables children to reveal their own perceptions is that of asking them to tell a story about the pictures they have drawn or about other art activity they have completed. Again, as we will discuss in the next chapter, you can have the child elaborate on any part of the drawing that you perceive to hold the most potential for self-revelation. "Tell me more about why the father was so mad." "Why did the boy tear up those pictures?" "What did that girl think about God?"

Creating a Title

Art therapists find it very helpful to have children give a title or name to each work, because the title can be so revealing. You can do the same by pointing out to the children that all artists give titles or names to their work. Their choice may be a significant clue to a central theme in their mind. After the child chooses a title and writes it on the work, you can ask, "Tell me how (or why) you decided on that title (name)," which could uncover rich information about what is going on in the child's life.

Alone or in Families?

Working with children in private gives them the opportunity to share things with you, the pastor, that they might not feel comfortable expressing within earshot of a parent or a sibling. It is important to have this individual time.

However, when parents or siblings are willing and interested, you can include as many family members as available in the process you are using. They will reveal things to each other that can be very helpful to the family as they deal with the crisis. Your skill in eliciting thoughts and feelings can accomplish the goals of helping the family deal with things realistically, reduce the amount of protection occurring, call forth empathy which will lead to supportive interaction, and establish the mutuality that can bond families together in a critical situation.

7

STORYTELLING
AND PASTORAL CARE

All human beings are created with the capacity for imagination. The ability has been all but squeezed out of many adults, but thank goodness children are able to fantasize about life. Imagination is necessary for learning and crucial for endowing life with meaning. Faith would be impossible without imagination. Furthermore, imagination is necessary for hope to exist, since hope is related to those things "we do not see" (Rom. 8:24–25).

A major way in which human beings express their imagination is through stories. The stories we tell may be based on fact, or they may grow out of fantasies about "what might have been" in the past or "what could be" in the future. Human beings have always used stories to preserve and communicate basic things about their cultural values, specifically their religious faith. Myths, legends, fables, and parables are the main vehicles by which religious people pass on to their children the central truths of their spiritual experience.

Story and Religion

One of the startling, yet refreshing, developments in the field of New Testament study has to do with the importance of the Gospel narratives, the stories themselves, in providing the major meanings of the gospel.[40] In theological studies, attention to "narrative theology" has put new emphasis on the significance of both the telling and the hearing of the biblical stories.[41]

Pastoral counseling has taken note of this emphasis on "story" and begun to point out the significance of an individual's life story.[42] The stories that a person tells about his or her life make up a history of that person's self-perceptions, regardless of the *objective* reality of the stories. The *subjective* reality is what gives meaning to that person's life. The subjective reality, with its assigned meanings, can be a central focus for pastoral psychotherapy. Understanding this story may be the key to helping a person change parts of it in order to pursue a more abundant life.

Awareness of the fact that we human beings build our lives around stories will motivate us to study more thoroughly the importance of stories in the growth and development of children. John Westerhoff, writing about nurturing faith in children, describes the importance of story in a child's faith.

> At every point in our lives, we seek and need to discover some meaning. The whole process begins at childhood when we learn through stories. . . . What is important for us to remember is that children and adults need to hear stories. It is human nature to order our lives in accordance with a story. . . . Stories provide our imaginations with the means for ordering our experiences. They leave us open to new insights and inspirations. Stories preserve the memory of past events and the experiences of the race in a way that allows those events and experiences to help shape our lives.[43]

For this reason, Westerhoff, discussing the significance of sharing our faith with our children, gives as his first guideline, "We need to tell and retell the biblical story—the stories of the faith."[44]

An example of the impact of the biblical story on a child's spiritual pilgrimage is described in a personal reflection by R. Alan Culpepper, associate professor of New Testament Interpretation, during a Faculty Address at the Southern Baptist Theological Seminary.

My Christian faith began in the first naivete, at the age of six. My father was reading the gospel story of the crucifixion. The story spoke to me of Jesus' love for the world, for me. The story of his suffering love was so powerful that it altered my perception of life irrevocably.[45]

Culpepper's father, Hugo H. Culpepper, a former missionary in China and South America and, until retirement, professor of Christian Missions and World Religions at the same seminary, had written an extensive account of this event in Alan's life. Alan Culpepper quotes the following from his father's description:

Alan's eyes filled with tears as he was visibly moved; he said, "Daddy, I just can't understand it—I try to, but I just can't." I explained to him that I did not understand all about it either, but that it made plain to us the love of God and the reality of sin. . . . A few days later . . . he came in and climbed up in my lap. He said, "Daddy, you know all those Bible stories we have been reading—well, I want you to tell me the *meaning* of them." I began and told him the story of creation and the fall and redemption on through the meaning of church membership and the ordinances.[46]

Then Alan Culpepper describes his response to hearing these stories of the faith which his father had both *read* to him and now had *told* him. "The following night I told my parents that I wanted to be baptized. I began a response, a commitment to live in response to Jesus as I had experienced him in the gospel story."[47] Then he describes the intervening years filled with academic pursuits as a New Testament scholar with particular interest in understanding the historical context of the New Testament period and claiming the historicity of the Gospels. Then Culpepper closes with this proclamation:

I now see that the gospels themselves contain the truth that matters. They put us in touch with Jesus the Christ, which is more important then the extent to which they may also put us in touch with the historical Jesus. . . . So

I call upon colleagues and students in both classroom and pulpit to "tell the old, old story of Jesus and his love," for there is more truth in that story than in any historical account we may reconstruct or any statement of doctrine we may devise.[48]

You can see the way in which stories can spark the imagination, call forth identification, and contribute to the choice of life's meaning for even young children.

A second example of the impact that biblical stories can have on children is reported by one of the respondents in James Fowler's well-known *Stages of Faith.*

One of our adult respondents, a male in his thirties, recalls that as a four-year-old he was required to take an afternoon nap. At the beginning of these naps his mother would sometimes read a story from the Bible. After reading the stories and responding to some of his curious questions, she would leave him "to go to sleep." Sleep came, he says, less frequently than rich fantasies and daydreams, often stimulated by the stories. . . . This man shared [a story about his childhood which] centered on his hearing the account of Samuel's call in the temple (I Sam. 1–3). As his mother told him the story of the dedication by Hannah of her son Samuel to the work of God, it made a strong impression on him. . . . He felt, he said, a special closeness to the boy Samuel as he served in the temple. . . . Later in his childhood and adolescence, this man says, he would frequently awaken in the middle of the night and in the pregnant darkness would find himself feeling, "Speak, Lord, for Thy servant hears." It comes as no surprise to learn that today he is a minister and theologian.[49]

Though his story begins at four years of age, a year earlier than the stage we are considering in this book, its influence on the spiritual formation of this man is evident.

We know that children in crisis are open to new learnings. They give interpretations, often religious interpretations, to the events and happenings that make up a crisis. When we use stories, biblical and otherwise, in our pastoral care, we give the children another vehicle for gaining insight and finding meaning in the crisis which contributes creatively to their spiritual pilgrimage.

TELLING BIBLE STORIES

As indicated above, telling stories to children is a method of sharing with them new and different perspectives on life, a goal of pastoral care with children. Telling biblical stories accomplishes this within the particular framework of our Judeo-Christian heritage. Through these stories we pass on our faith by giving children the opportunity (1) to use our heritage as the context for processing their response to a crisis, and by helping them (2) to make religious interpretations and gain spiritual insights from within this same tradition.

Stories About Jesus and the Children

Can you imagine how exciting it is for a child to hear you carefully tell the story about Jesus rebuking the disciples for trying to keep people from bringing the children into his presence (Mark 10:13–14)? Reading it makes for a short story, but telling it with some true-to-the-story details, and some history about the blessings of religious leaders, holds the child enthralled. Then you can ask some questions of the child, or children if you are with several siblings or a special group, which will draw forth interesting comments: "Why did the people want Jesus to bless the children?" "I wonder why the disciples tried to stop them?" "Why do you think Jesus got upset with them?" "What do you think the children wanted to talk to Jesus about?" You can imagine what the answers to these questions could reveal about what a child in crisis was thinking and feeling. The questions can be suited to the age of the child. As the conversation moves along, you have a chance to state some truths concerning how Jesus feels about children, which the child will not forget.

The story of the young boy with the loaves and fish (John

6:5–14) gives you an opportunity to discuss the contributions that children can make when there is a problem, plus the importance of serving those in need. As we said earlier, children often feel left out when there is a crisis. This story can give them an opportunity to share those feelings.

Stories About Crises

Certain biblical stories give children an opportunity to think about specific crises they have experienced. The story of Jesus' grief over the death of his friend Lazarus (John 11:1–44) enables children to hear about, then talk about, bereavement. Your questions would focus on the grief: "I wonder what Jesus was thinking when he heard that Lazarus was dead?" "Why did Jesus cry?" "Why did Jesus want to see him after he was dead?" "What did Jesus want to do next?" Again, you can imagine how this story provides a grieved child with an opportunity to talk indirectly about his or her own grief.

A storm on the Sea of Galilee frightened the disciples (Mark 4:35–41) and they thought they were going to die. Jesus calmed the waves, but, more important, he quieted the disciples. His question, "Why are you afraid?" is a good one to ask children in crisis. "What do you think the disciples were worried about?" "When were you last afraid of something?" "What does it mean to be brave?" "Is being brave something like having faith?" These further questions allow the children to discuss fear.

RELATING TO CHILDREN THROUGH STORYTELLING

Because children enjoy both hearing and telling stories, storytelling is one of the common techniques used by counselors and psychotherapists who work with children. When children tell stories, they reveal important information about their inner thoughts and feelings. To the careful observer, stories make known the thought processes and the images by which the children are making sense out of their world. They also reveal the emotional world of children—the fears, hopes, and guilts which accompany their perceptions. The younger children in our age group (those five to nine) are unaware that so much of their selfhood is contained in their stories; therefore they are largely unselfconscious about participating in storytelling. They do not consciously censor what they say in fear that they will say something they should not, as begins to happen around nine years of age. Many ten- to twelve-year-olds still enjoy storytelling, but they are more aware of what they are revealing about themselves.

Therapists, as we have pointed out earlier, are not the only ones interested in knowing about a child's inner thoughts and feelings. Giving pastoral care to children in crisis can be most effective when we know how they are interpreting these specific events in their lives. Listening to a child's story, or the child's response to a story you tell or read, can serve as an excellent tool for pastoral assessment.

I find three differences between the pastoral use of stories and the normal way a psychotherapist works with them. First, most therapists do not tell stories themselves. They are interested only in what the child reveals and may feel that for them, as therapists, to tell stories would influence what the child tells, thereby keeping the child from revealing the unconscious material for which the therapist is looking. As a pastor, however, caring for children outside a formal, long-term, once-a-week therapy session, I find it most helpful to join with the child in storytelling. Children are more likely to participate when I invite them to join me in something that we will do together than when I ask them to "perform" for me. So instead of saying to a child, "Tell me a story," it is more likely that I will say, "One thing we can do is tell stories to each other. Why don't you be first?" The child, or children if there are several involved, may want to find out more about my proposal, but already knows I am not asking him or her to do something I will not do myself.

A second difference has to do with the type of structure one might use. A therapist knows that both conscious and unconscious information will be exposed by the child's story; therefore the therapist will usually allow the child to tell a story without giving any guidelines. When you, the pastor, are car-

ing for a child in crisis, this same approach may be quite sufficient. When you ask children to tell you a story, you can let
them tell any story they desire without guidelines from you. If
a child asks, "What should we tell stories about?" you can
answer, "Anything we want to."

At other times, however, because you want to focus the
child's attention on a particular subject or event in the child's
life, you will find it more helpful to give some instructions:
"Well, why don't we tell stories about sad things that happen
to people?" "Tell a story about some animal that got scared."

A third difference has to do with the therapist's willingness
to impart specific values to the child. Most therapists do not
think it appropriate to impart their value system to their pa-
tients even though they are trying to help them attain a higher
degree of mental health and emotional well-being. They are
more interested in receiving information from the child in
order to make an accurate diagnosis than in trying to provide
information for the child.

An exception is Richard Gardner, the noted child psychiatrist mentioned in chapter 5. He points out that many techniques used by child psychotherapists "are based on the assumption, borrowed from the adult psychoanalytic model, that
making the unconscious conscious can itself be therapeutic."
He goes on to say, "My own experience has revealed that few
children are interested in gaining conscious awareness of their
unconscious processes, let alone utilizing such insights
therapeutically."[50] So how can the child be helped to change
and grow? Gardner began to realize the potential of storytelling for communicating values and insights to children.[51] From
this observation he developed the Mutual Storytelling Technique,[52] to which we will return later in the chapter.

The purpose of pastoral care not only includes learning
about the child but also includes looking for opportunities to
guide and direct, even correct, a child's perceptions. We are
interested in having children adopt a value system. Knowing
that stories have the capacity to provide grist for the child's
imaginative mill, we tell or read stories to children with the
purpose of making a point. To do so is a valid pastoral care
function.

INVOLVING CHILDREN IN STORYTELLING

You may be wondering, How in the world do you motivate a child to tell a story? It is not as hard as it seems.

Using Play and Art

One possibility is the use of techniques that we described in chapters 5 and 6. When playing the Ungame, for example, landing on a "do your own thing" square allows you to ask a question of any other player. This gives you an opportunity to say, "I want Tony to tell a story about new baby brothers," or some other topic that would allow the child to deal with a crisis. Remember that the Bag of Words game is centered around storytelling. Using this game provides plenty of impetus for storytelling. Remember, put words in the bag about which you think it would be most helpful for you and the child to tell stories. If you use puppets, children find it quite easy to let their puppets tell stories and they like to listen to your puppet tell stories. We have already described how art work provides an excellent focus for storytelling, because children enjoy telling stories about things they have created. Any of the drawings mentioned in chapter 6 would serve as an opportunity to ask a child to tell a story.

Person-on-the-Street Interviews

Another excellent prop is a tape recorder. Many children have never heard their voice on a tape recorder, even though many homes have one. Regardless, children like to hear themselves speaking. Most children have seen on the "Muppet Show" and on "Sesame Street" those make-believe person-on-the-street interviews or people-in-the-news stories to which they respond so positively.

Ask the child to play this game with you by first describing it and asking if he or she has ever seen such a program. If the child has not, you can elaborate. Then suggest that you will be the news reporter first and then the child can have a turn. Start the tape recorder, hold the microphone up to your mouth, and introduce the program.

> Hello, ladies and gentlemen, welcome to our people-in-
> the-news program. We have with us today [hold the
> microphone in front of the child and indicate with a nod
> that he or she should answer]. We understand, [name],
> that you have witnessed a major news story today. Please
> tell our audience about your experience.

As the child tells the news story, you can shape your questions
to draw out thoughts and feelings about the make-believe
events.

The child can be directed specifically to the crisis at hand.
You may ask, "You, [name], have recently visited your
mother in the hospital, please give us a report." This allows
you to follow up with questions such as, "How are things at
home while your mother is in the hospital?"

Mutual Storytelling Technique

Richard Gardner gives an excellent model for inviting children to tell stories when he invites them to participate on his
"Dr. Gardner's 'Make-Up-a-Story Television Program.' "[53]
He has a fully equipped office, of course, including video
cameras, tape recorders, and television monitors which most of
us do not have. When adapting his model to my situation, I first
invite the child, or children if in a group, to be on my make-
believe radio broadcast. Usually the child agrees readily, so I
set the scene with a tape recorder, turn it on, and say (following Gardner):

> Good morning, boys and girls, I'd like to welcome you
> once again to Dr. Lester's "Make-Up-a-Story Radio Pro-
> gram." We know that children are good at making up
> exciting stories, so we invite children to our program to
> tell stories. Remember now, it is against the rules to tell
> a story you have heard from someone else, or seen on
> television, or read in a book. Every story on this program
> must be your own story, made up by your own brain.
>   Another thing to remember. A story should have a
> beginning, a middle, and an end. After you tell the story,
> you will tell us the moral or lesson of the story.
>   When each child is through with his or her story, I will

make up a story, too. And when I finish, I will tell the moral of my story also.

And now, without further delay, let me introduce to you a girl (boy) who is with us today for the first time. Will you please tell us your name, young lady (man)?

I then ask a series of information questions that put the child at ease. Then I can say, "Now we are ready to hear your story." If the child seems stuck, I mention (following Gardner) that although there are many stories in every child's head, it is not always easy to think of one when you are on the program for the first time. Then I offer to help the child. If the child accepts, I can say:

> I will start the story and when I point to you, you can say the first thing that comes to your mind. Then it will be easy to make up the rest. Okay, let's start. Once upon a time, in a faraway land, there lived a _____.

When I point toward the child, it is usually easy for the child to fill in the blank. If the child does not continue, I can continue with, "and that (boy, girl, family, horse, etc.) had _____ _____." Again, I point to the child, who may continue the story or may need a few more "starter" statements from me which allow him or her to fill in the blanks. When the child finishes the story, he or she is asked to give the story a title or a name and then to tell the audience the main moral, or lesson, from the story.

As the story is told, and the title and lesson described, I listen carefully for the primary meanings revealed. What are the child's concerns, fears, or anxieties? How is the child interpreting the crisis? Does this interpretation need correcting? What theological/spiritual conclusions is the child reaching? Are they adequate or do they need filling out? The second step, after thanking the child for the story, is to ask any questions about the story that will help me understand what the child is communicating and allow the child to share even more. Questions like: "What was the little girl thinking when _____ _____?" "Why did the father _____?" or "Explain to me what _____ means."

The third step is for me to tell a story. My story will normally include the same characters and be placed in the same context as the child's story, except that my story will include different happenings and perhaps a different ending than the child's, depending on what new information or possibilities about life the child needs to hear. Then I give my story a title and describe the main moral or lesson.

At this point I may choose to discuss the stories and the lessons with the child. At other times I may decide that the telling of the stories has been sufficient for allowing the child to share what he or she is experiencing and for giving me a chance to make input to the child's perception and offer new insights.

CHILDREN'S LITERATURE

An excellent resource for pastoral care of children through storytelling is children's literature. Many good books for children deal with subject matter that causes stress for children—death, divorce, separation, imprisonment, failure, and so forth.

Children love to listen to stories. As pastor, you can choose to read a story that addresses a crisis which one or more of the children have experienced. Then you can ask questions such as those we have illustrated earlier. This gives the children an opportunity to conceptualize and express their inner thoughts and feelings.

We will not discuss particular children's books that you can use for this purpose. Your church librarian or someone who works in the children's section of the public library could be of help. Joan Fassler has written an excellent book, *Helping Children Cope,* which describes and evaluates a number of children's books that can be used in helping children cope with crises.[54]

8

PASTORAL CARE
THROUGH WRITING

Written words have a different reality than spoken words. Speaking and writing are not only different physical actions, they also engage different mental and psychological processes. To write and to speak about the same subject, let's say in response to a question, will produce, to some degree and in some manner, a different answer.

Spoken words have much power. Once uttered, words take on a life of their own. What they express can no longer be denied or fantasized, for they are now public property rather than private property. The speaker can now be held accountable and responsible for them. The thoughts and feelings captured and conveyed by the words must now be "owned" by the speaker. They can never be "taken back." This power and reality about words make people, *including children,* hesitant to verbalize about sensitive personal matters, particularly those which make them vulnerable.

The writing process seems to be less personal and less threatening. In pastoral counseling with adults, I often assign written "homework." I may have parishioners/clients write a letter to a long-dead parent about their stored up rage, describe on paper a fantasy about their spouse, or develop a written plan for solving a particular problem. Often these persons are able to conceptualize ideas, reveal personal history, and express intensity of emotion which was not possible for them to "speak." The act of writing was somehow a less threatening mode of communication with me than the spoken word.

The written word, however, carries its own unique vitality —namely, the power to permit the unspeakable to become speakable. Once written down, the ideas, thoughts, and feelings behind words are often less frightening. Illustrating the Hebrew idea that by naming a thing a person gains power over it, parishioners/clients often feel more free to converse with me about private things after they have written about them. The act of writing breaks through the internal barriers erected by the fear of perceived dangers in the spoken word.

I learned in an earlier research project[55] that writing allowed adolescents to express things on paper through diaries, guided essays, and sentence completions which they found difficult to verbalize. Yet, after writing the words, they were comfortable pursuing the subjects in pastoral conversation. I find the same thing to be true of children.

As we have said before, children are aware of the power of words, particularly the impact that spoken words have on adults. Therefore, children are quite careful about the vocabulary they use around adults, including the pastor. Furthermore, if children become aware that certain topics (death, sex, body functions, divorce, etc.) and certain emotions (anger, sadness, fear) upset the adults in their lives, they protect themselves by avoiding these subjects and feelings.

The process of writing, however, seems to give permission to children to share themselves on otherwise taboo subjects. The child's internal censor does not perceive the written word to be as dangerous as the spoken word and permits, therefore, more free expression of the child's real self.

Since the written word and the spoken word have different meanings in our culture, pastoral care is enhanced by using the written word as an adjunct to pastoral conversation with children. Younger children, of course, cannot write and would find it difficult to respond in this manner. They do understand writing, however, and are often glad to dictate some story or letter to an adult who volunteers to write it down for them. Older children, however, from around eight years of age and increasing in age, can participate in writing activities. We will describe below four types of writing activity that pastors can use in their ministry with children.

FINISHING SENTENCES

Older children will tell you many things by the way they complete open-ended sentences. You are probably familiar with the sentence completion technique used in psychological testing. A number of sentences are begun on the left side of a page, each one containing a key word or phrase that leads the child to reflect on feelings, values, hopes, self-perceptions, needs, family relationships, philosophy, and religion. As children finish these sentences, they are usually providing spontaneous reflections about their inner thoughts and feelings.

The child psychologist will use these reflections as clues to understanding the inner world of the child. As a pastor, of course, you are not trying to make formal diagnoses but are simply trying to learn as much as you can about how children view their particular crisis so that you can provide carefully planned pastoral care.

Preparation

The pastor can develop a master list of sentence completion possibilities from which to choose the appropriate ones for a given child. Some of the categories, and some examples of specific sentence completions that can be very revealing, are listed here.

Feelings   I feel sad
       I get angry
       I am glad when
       It sure is lonely
       Crying is
       It was embarrassing
       Everybody was excited when
       I hate
       I felt really bad
       I would be happy if

Values	I don't think people should
	Nice people always
	I hope I never
	I would feel terrible if
	My parents taught me that
	I feel good when I
	If I had lots of money
	Children should
Hopes	When I grow up
	I hope Mom
	Maybe next year
	If only I could
	I wonder if
	From now on
Self-perceptions	If I could change my body, I would
	Girls think I
	I wish I was
	One thing I do best is
	I'm working hard to
	I just can't
	What I like most about myself is
	I'm different from other children because
	At school I
	Boys think I
Needs	I wish I had
	I sure need
	When I talk
	If I could just
	I wish Dad
	I can't believe
Family relationships	My father always
	Sisters should
	My mother usually
	If my brother

My family doesn't
Mother and I

Philosophy	I think God
and	After dying
religion	Death means
	I wish God
	When I'm at church
	When I pray
	I always wondered why
	I worry about
	I am thankful that
	I want to know
	I don't understand why

Of course you would not use all of these at one time. When planning to work with a specific child, you can indicate a select list of ten to twenty sentence completions from your master list which could be typed nicely on one sheet of paper. Choose the ones that will provide an opportunity for this particular child to reveal the thoughts and feelings which you imagine to be most important in the child's crisis. You can add some sentence completions around the specific theme of this child's crisis:

After Daddy and Mommy divorced
When Grandpa died
After we move, I think
I think this disease
Being sick means

Structuring
Using sentence completions will be less threatening and therefore more effective if they come after a pastoral relationship has been established. Even though sentence completion is not as threatening as verbalization, it still demands a trusting relationship which is already characterized by open communication and sharing. This method is not good to break the ice

or to establish the relationship. Play and art activities are much better in the early stages.

At some appropriate point the pastor can say, "We've gotten to know each other quite well. We've played games, drawn pictures, and told stories. Another thing we could do together is finish sentences. Would you like to do it?" When the child agrees, simple instructions usually suffice. I have found it helpful to give some examples on scratch paper or on the back of the sheet. "This is how you do it. If I wrote, 'The horse is going . . . ,' how would you finish that sentence?" After several such examples, the child will know what you want. Then hand the child the paper and say, "I've begun some sentences on this sheet of paper. Read the first words and then finish them in any way you want."

When the child is through, read over the completions and thank the child for sharing so much with you. Then you may ask the child to help you understand certain of the sentences as a way of engaging in pastoral conversation. Gary, a twelve-year-old with a life-threatening blood disease, can serve as an example of such conversation. I asked, "Gary, tell me more about this sentence you completed which reads, 'I always wonder why God is doing this to me.' " He proceeded to tell me of a recent visit from his grandmother, who had told him during her visit that God was trying to teach him a lesson through this illness. He liked and respected his grandmother and had been trying to figure out what lesson God was trying to teach him. Our conversation led toward my realization that Gary was wrestling with the question of causation. That is, did God *cause* this illness to teach him something or was God preparing to teach him something from a disease that came from somewhere else? Pursuing this question led us to discuss how God felt about this life-threatening illness. Gary came to believe that God was for him, not against him! All in all, it was a very significant pastoral conversation which grew out of this sentence completion method.

If a child enjoys the sentence completions, you can always take another set at a later time. With children eight to ten years of age you might call this the Sentence Finishing game, but with the older ones you can simply talk about "finishing sentences as a way of getting to know each other."

Sometimes sentence completions can be given to a child as an assignment to be done before your next visit. Or you can ask the child to finish it sometime that day and mail it to you (provide the self-addressed, stamped envelope). Most of the time it should be done while you are there so the conversation about it takes place while the child's thinking process is fresh.

The Pastor's Participation

As indicated earlier, children are uncomfortable if you sit and stare while they are working. You might suggest that while the child is finishing the sentences, you will be drawing a picture (if the two of you have done this before), or reading an article you have to read today (then sit nearby and read until the child finishes), or, if you are at your office, working with the secretary (step out until the child has enough time to finish).

Pastoral care can be offered through your participation in a different way. After the child is familiar with sentence completions, you can tell the child that you will finish any five of the sentences which he or she might choose for you to complete, either during that session or at a later visit. Imaginative children may even create some special sentence completions for you. They may choose sentences for you to finish which raise the important issues about which they have been thinking. How you finish them might give you the opportunity to "correct" a distortion or at least offer another way of viewing a situation. For example, a ten-year-old boy, Fred, of divorced parents, living with his mother and visiting his father every other weekend, completed the phrase, "I think my father . . . " with the words "doesn't want to be with me anymore." He chose to ask me to finish the same phrase, which I did with the words, "is confused about how to relate to Fred." Then when he asked me what I meant by "confused," I shared my perception that his father wanted to spend time with him but was also trying to give attention to a new family. I also shared that since he and his dad got into conflict during their last several visits, the father was wondering whether Fred was enjoying the visits and really wanted to come. This led into some pastoral conversation about their conflict and how Fred could communicate to his dad what he felt.

STORIES

As described in chapter 7, children enjoy telling stories and reveal much about themselves when they do. Here we point out that older children who may feel too self-conscious to *tell* stories will often *write* stories for you that might help you understand their situation.

Children like to help other people, so one way I have approached the assignment can be illustrated by my pastoral use of story with Andrea, a twelve-year-old whose parents recently divorced.

> Andrea, I'm working with some other children a little younger than you whose parents are going to get a divorce. I am trying to prepare them for what it will be like to go through this experience. I need your help. Would you take time this week to write a story about what a child feels and thinks when parents divorce? It only needs to be a couple of pages long. Then I can read your story to these other children. It will really help them figure out what is going on.

When Andrea wrote her story, several good things happened. First, since Andrea automatically made the story autobiographical, it helped her to express some of what she had experienced. Second, I was able to engage her in conversation about some portions of the story which enabled me to broaden my perspective on her experience. Third, I have a good story to read to other children who go through the same crisis.

Later, I wanted to check out Andrea's religious perceptions, so I asked, as a specific part of the assignment, "These children have asked me specific questions about what God thinks of this whole matter, so please include in your story something about how God is involved." When she finished, her story revealed her perceptions of God's activity in the world which I could confirm at points and attempted to modify at other points to strengthen her spiritual pilgrimage.

Another good use of stories is asking children with whom you have done art work to write stories about their pictures. Children will often express significant aspects of their crisis when following such an assignment. This can often be done between visits and gives a clear structure for the next conversation.

DIARIES

Older children who have learned to express themselves through the written word may keep a diary for you. It would be understood that the diary would be intended for your eyes only and represent a covenant concerning your interest in learning what the child was experiencing during a particular stressful time in life. You could ask the child to write each night some of the most important things that had gone through her or his mind during that day. When you read the diary at your next visit, you can ask for elaboration on the child's thoughts and feelings.

POETRY

Some older children will write poetry for you. At certain stages they get interested in poems and rhymes. My daughter is eleven years old and recently finished a written project entitled "Thoughts, Feelings, and Everything Else Inside" for a school class. She has included some poetry that is quite self-revealing. If she were in a crisis, a thoughtful pastor could ask her to express her experience in a poem.

If a child responds positively to your question, "Do you like poems?" ask the child to write you a poem about one of the following: "What is going on inside you?" "What is it like when a brother dies?" "How does it feel to be so sad?" The act of reflecting and expressing is in itself of help to the child who takes your challenge.

EPILOGUE

Now you are wondering what to do with all these new ideas. Perhaps you are thinking of a specific child in your parish who is in a crisis situation. You are excited, it is hoped, about the possibilities of caring for children, even though it may feel risky. In case you have any doubts about whether spending the time to care for children is worthwhile, let me share a thought from Clark Moustakas:

> In each life, there are moments that leave an imprint in the mind and heart and spirit, moments that transcend lesser times and enable a person to stretch beyond what he [she] has known, into a new realm of discovery. . . . The existential moment is sometimes the beginning of a new conviction or commitment emerging from a distinctive and particular identity. Such moments provide substance for searching, struggling, feeling, asserting, yielding, facing and choosing a direction that challenges and enhances realization of potentialities both in the individual and in his [her] growing relationships. . . . A real person emerges who is suddenly present in the world, ready to collaborate with life, ready to use his [her] resources for self-growth and for fundamental ties to nature and the universe.[56]

And we would add, this child is preparing to encounter God. Yes, you can be the midwife for such a moment in a child's life. By offering a stable relationship characterized by acceptance, love, and care, you can provide a powerful, redemptive environment in which such an encounter can occur.

Finally, I want to share my excitement about what caring for children can mean to you. I have been significantly blessed by the children to whom I have ministered. Though they remain largely unaware of their contributions to my life, they have often functioned in both a priestly ("Are you sad today, Rev. Lester?") and a prophetic ("I don't know what that word means!") manner. Their sharp minds, probing questions, open hearts, unique insights, fresh faith, and unfailing hope never fail to undergird my own faith and stretch the spiritual dimensions of my awareness. I see more clearly why Jesus rebuked the disciples for keeping the children away from him. I guarantee that once you get past the level of superficiality and overcome the anxiety, caring for children will become a joyful endeavor. Instead of dreading such encounters, you will anticipate them as a source of personal renewal.

NOTES

1. For a new perspective on shepherding as a model for pastors, see Alastair V. Campbell, *Rediscovering Pastoral Care* (Westminster Press, 1981), pp. 36–45.

2. For a detailed study, see Hans-Ruedi Weber, *Jesus and the Children* (John Knox Press, 1980).

3. See Ashley Montagu, *Touching: The Human Significance of the Skin* (Columbia University Press, 1971).

4. For a careful study of "blessing," see Myron C. Madden, *The Power to Bless* (Abingdon Press, 1970).

5. See this concern discussed in John H. Westerhoff, *Will Our Children Have Faith?* (Seabury Press, 1976).

6. Wayne E. Oates, *On Becoming Children of God* (Westminster Press, 1969), p. 11.

7. Ibid.

8. Ibid., p. 12.

9. See Carroll A. Wise, *The Meaning of Pastoral Care* (Harper & Row, 1966).

10. Benjamin T. Griffin, "Pastoral Care of Children in Crisis" (unpublished D. Min. project, Lancaster Theological Seminary, 1975), pp. 10–11.

11. Ibid., p. 11.

12. Ibid., p. 12.

13. David K. Switzer, *The Minister as Crisis Counselor* (Abingdon Press, 1974), p. 23.

14. Ibid., pp. 20–28.

15. For more information about children's stress, see David Elkind, *The Hurried Child: Growing Up Too Fast Too Soon* (Addison-Wesley Publishing Co., 1981), particularly Ch. 7.

16. Daniel Day Williams, *The Minister and the Care of Souls* (Harper & Row, 1961), p. 26.

17. See Gordon W. Allport, *Pattern and Growth in Personality* (Holt, Rinehart & Winston, 1961).

18. Wayne E. Oates, *The Christian Pastor,* 3d ed., revised (Westminster Press, 1982), p. 22.

19. Including child psychiatrists, child psychologists, psychoanalysts, social workers, pediatric nurses, child guidance counselors, child developmentalists, and other mental health professionals.

20. For a thorough discussion of children in the preadolescent stage of life, see the textbook by Joyce Wolfgang Williams and Marjorie Smith, *Middle Childhood: Behavior and Development,* 2d ed. (Macmillan Publishing Co., 1980). An easy-to-read introduction would be B. Max Price, *Understanding Today's Children* (Convention Press, 1982). For an excellent look at the uniqueness of women's development, see Carol Gilligan, *In a Different Voice: Psychological Theory and Women's Development* (Harvard University Press, 1982).

21. Erik H. Erikson, *Childhood and Society,* 2d ed., revised and enlarged (W. W. Norton & Co., 1964), pp. 258–261.

22. Robert J. Havighurst, *Developmental Tasks and Education,* 3d ed. (David McKay Co., 1972), p. 34.

23. Ibid.

24. Oates, *The Christian Pastor,* p. 194. See also Martin E. Marty, *Friendship* (Argus Communications, 1980), for an excellent discussion on the nature of friendship, most of which is applicable to adult-child relationships.

25. Oates, *The Christian Pastor,* p. 197.

26. Iris V. Cully, *Christian Child Development* (Harper & Row,

1979), summarizes most of the important studies in cognitive, moral, and faith development and applies these concepts to Christian education.

27. For an excellent discussion of how this is done, see William L. Hendricks, *A Theology for Children* (Broadman Press, 1980). For the most complete study of cognitive and psychosocial development related to faith stages, see James W. Fowler, *Stages of Faith: The Psychology of Human Development and the Quest for Meaning* (Harper & Row, 1981).

28. See Erik H. Erikson, *Toys and Reasons: Stages in the Ritualization of Experience* (W. W. Norton & Co., 1977).

29. For an overview of different approaches to play therapy, see Jessie Oliver James, *Play Therapy: An Overview* (Joel Mandel Books, 1977). Other excellent books on play therapy include Garry L. Landreth, ed., *Play Therapy: Dynamics of the Process of Counseling with Children* (Charles C. Thomas, 1982), and Charles E. Schaefer, ed., *The Therapeutic Use of Child's Play* (Jason Aronson, 1976).

30. For a beautiful story of a child's self-discovery through play therapy, see Virginia M. Axline, *Dibs: In Search of Self* (Houghton Mifflin Co., 1964).

31. For examples of facilitating a child's self-expression, see Clark E. Moustakas, ed., *The Child's Discovery of Himself* (Jason Aronson, 1973).

32. Ungame is produced by The Ungame Co., Anaheim, Calif., and available in many Christian bookstores.

33. Richard A. Gardner, *Psychotherapy with Children of Divorce* (Jason Aronson, 1976), pp. 70–76. His "Talking, Feeling and Doing Game" (pp. 81–86) is also an excellent vehicle for pastoral conversation.

34. For understanding art therapy, see Edith Kramer and Laurie Wilson, *Childhood and Art Therapy: Notes on Theory and Application* (Schocken Books, 1980).

35. For examples, see Margaret Naumburg, *An Introduction to Art Therapy,* rev. ed. (Teachers College Press, 1973).

36. See examples in Elinor Ulman and Penny Dachinger, eds., *Art Therapy in Theory and Practice* (Schocken Books, 1976).

37. Claudia L. Jewett, *Helping Children Cope with Separation and Loss* (Harvard Common Press, 1982), pp. 55–57.

38. For an excellent, practical, easy-to-read discussion of separation and loss in children, see Jewett, *Helping Children Cope.*

39. For therapeutic techniques in using art with families, see Hanna Y. Kwiatkowska, *Family Therapy and Evaluation Through Art* (Charles C. Thomas, 1978).

40. See Walter Wink, *The Bible in Human Transformation* (Fortress Press, 1973).

41. See Michael Goldberg, *Theology and Narrative: A Critical Introduction* (Abingdon Press, 1982).

42. See Charles Gerkin, *The Living Human Document: Revisioning Pastoral Counseling in a Hermeneutical Mode* (Abingdon Press, 1984).

43. John H. Westerhoff, *Bringing Up Children in the Christian Faith* (Winston Press, 1980), pp. 39–40.

44. Ibid., p. 36.

45. R. Alan Culpepper, "Story and History in the Gospels," *Review and Expositor,* Vol. 81, No. 3 (Summer 1984), p. 476.

46. Ibid.

47. Ibid., pp. 476–477.

48. Ibid., p. 477. For R. Alan Culpepper's work with "story" in the New Testament, see his *Anatomy of the Fourth Gospel: A Study in Literary Design* (Fortress Press, 1983).

49. Fowler, *Stages of Faith,* pp. 130–131.

50. Gardner, *Psychotherapy with Children of Divorce,* p. 57.

51. Ibid., p. 58.

52. Richard A. Gardner, *Therapeutic Communication with Children: The Mutual Storytelling Technique* (Science House, 1971).

53. Gardner, *Psychotherapy with Children of Divorce,* pp. 58–59.

54. Joan Fassler, *Helping Children Cope* (Free Press, 1978).

55. Andrew D. Lester, "Implications of the Needs and Experiences of Selected Adolescents for the Church's Ministry" (unpublished Ph.D. dissertation, Southern Baptist Theological Seminary, Louisville, Ky., 1967).

56. Moustakas, *The Child's Discovery of Himself,* pp. 1–2.

INDEX